THE APOSTATE'S CREED

'Is it the gods who put this desire into our minds, or does every person's irresistible passion become their god'?

Publius Vergilius Maro, (Virgil),
The Aeneid, Book 9. C1stBCE

lendwithcare

THE APOSTATE'S CREED

Rethinking Christianity for the C21st

Ben Whitney

A CIP catalogue record for this book is available from the British Library.

ISBN 978-0-9569568-6-6

Book and cover design by Clare Brayshaw

Prepared and printed by:

York Publishing Services Ltd
64 Hallfield Road
Layerthorpe
York YO31 7ZQ
Tel: 01904 431213

Website: www.yps-publishing.co.uk

CONTENTS

INTRODUCTION

'The great myths show that when you follow somebody else's path, you go astray. The hero has to set off by himself, leaving the old world and the old ways behind. He must venture into the darkness of the unknown, where there is no map and no clear route. He must fight his own monsters, not somebody else's, explore his own labyrinth, and endure his own ordeal before he can find what is missing in his life. Thus transfigured he (or she) can then bring something of value to the world that is left behind.'

Karen Armstrong

"The Spiral Staircase", Harper (2005)

Part 1 of this book is an exploration of some selected phrases from the Apostles' Creed, one of the classic summaries of Christian faith, but by someone who no longer believes that most of what it says is true – hence the witty title! (I'm amazed that no-one seems to have used it before). Part 2 is a series of reflections; the 'virtual' sermons I would have preached if anyone had asked me to. They are a response to the Common Lectionary passages set during June to August 2019. My aim is to find something positive to say from within the Jesus story, even if they're not the usual sermons you'd expect to hear in most churches.

After an explanation of my somewhat ambiguous personal context and the rather labyrinthine 'spiritual' path that has brought me to here, there follows a brief historical scene-setter. Where did the Apostles' Creed come from? Books about what it means to believe it often miss this element out entirely. But the orthodox doctrines were defined a very long time ago by statements such as these. That's part of my problem with them. So my first task is to try to understand what the compilers of this and other Creeds thought they were doing, before I try to apply their claims to the C21st. All religions have a human story behind them and everything we now assume to be an integral part of them was at one time created from new. I am very interested in Christian history and would like to know a little more about the background and processes which led to these particular convictions that most people would now more or less take for granted as the essence of Christianity. Why did they affirm what they did?

However, this is not an academic or scholarly work. You won't find footnotes or lengthy quotations from the Church Fathers. It is a thoughtful tract; perhaps sometimes a rant in places, but not an objective investigation. It is meant to stimulate, even to provoke. I have little time for Christian writers who tie themselves up in knots trying to say something radical, (like there is no God), but in language that sounds as if they are still on-side. Or those who write in styles that are so opaque that they hope to avoid being thought too controversial. I can understand why they do it. They might just be trying to keep their jobs.

The Church has usually been very intolerant of those who have wanted to rock the theological boat. I have no such worries, but I don't under-estimate the challenge. Change comes rather slowly in Christianity. (It was only relatively recently that the Roman Catholic Church officially admitted it was wrong about Galileo and Copernicus. It will probably catch up on Darwin, contraception, women's rights and sexual abuse by priests eventually!)

This project might sound as if it will have to involve some wrestling with complex Greek or Latin terms. That certainly happened at the time. The Creeds weren't of course written in English; the word 'Creed' comes from the Latin 'Credo' – 'I believe'. I prefer to avoid such dull debates, the significance of which is now entirely lost. But no-one should jump immediately to their own interpretation of what the statements mean. They belong in their own time and place and we have to at least start there, even though, for example, the 'up' and 'down' images used to describe our alleged relationship to a Deity have clearly been overtaken by subsequent discoveries and cannot now be taken literally, even if that was what they thought then.

This historical perspective is essential for all study of ancient writings. The Bible also needs to be approached in this way, which many believers seem to find difficult. One of the most important, and perhaps surprising, points to make before we even start is that the classic Creeds contain no statement about 'believing in' the Bible, despite the reverence with which it is usually treated. The claim that the whole thing, every single word, is somehow inerrant and authoritative for all time is a very recent idea and not part of the historic content of orthodox belief. Indeed some people's treatment of it verges on 'bibliolatry' as if it is the object most to be worshipped and obeyed. It is impossible to see this view of the Bible as rationally justified, but that doesn't stop it happening.

Some churches have such assertions about the Bible at the very top of their entry requirements, even before anything about Jesus. It's a 'given', not up for discussion. Some believers seem to think that they only have to read it and let God 'speak', as if the words are nothing to do with those who wrote them. The most extreme even claim that God 'wrote' the Bible and so it is always 'true' (whatever they mean by that). That has no integrity for me. Just like the Creeds, the Bible too is a collection of human writings, not some mysterious book that fell from the sky. Everything is there for a particular reason, and it's not all the same kind of literature. It spans hundreds of years and the text exists in several variant versions. We don't actually have any original manuscripts anyway and not all of the many translations are necessarily accurate. Maybe the authors didn't know everything then that we know now, spiritually as well as scientifically.

So I will begin with the initial setting for the Apostles' Creed, as far as we know much about it. But then I want to take its statements on into whether they can still mean anything to people like me today who are in search of a new kind of 'humanist spirituality', if still within the Christian tradition. This life is all we get and we each have to make some sense of it. There is no underlying pre-determined meaning to be discovered, it has to be created. I come from an essentially rationalist perspective which sees all religion as a human language about life, not as a door into a greater truth that is 'outside' of us. If such a reality exists, we cannot, by definition, know it. I am faced with many of the same questions that religions claim to answer, but I am seeking new answers and new ways of understanding them. Much re-interpreting will be in store but I will try not to confuse my own ideas with those who came before me.

Although I still use the word like everyone else, there is really no such thing as 'Christianity', only 'Christianities', each of them defined by those who adopt a particular stance. All talk of God is contextual: (see for e.g. the writings of Stephen B. Bevans in Chicago). It is inevitably influenced by its time and setting. So surely all Creeds and statements of faith must be the same? This is the story that the New Testament reveals right from the word go, as an essentially Jewish beginning gave way to beliefs influenced by the Greek/Gentile world. It obviously didn't stop there, so why do we still include such ancient sources in our liturgies as if all we have to do is keep repeating them? We need to be constantly rethinking them. Beliefs change according to the perspectives of those who believe them, even if some may claim to be more authentic than others. There is a feminist theology, a liberation theology, a capitalist theology, a white supremacist theology and a nice middle class C of E on a Sunday morning theology! But is there also a set of core beliefs which cannot be changed, or is everything always up for grabs?

My own context is C21st 'secular' humanism, but I recognise that I am also in dialogue with ideas from other times and different contexts. I still seek to follow 'The

Way' of Jesus. More of that later, especially in Chapter 4 and Part 2. And of course I am not the first to undertake this journey. One of my companions, (though I don't know that he would have wanted to come, had I been able to ask him), is the New Testament scholar Professor C.E.B. Cranfield, who died in 2015 aged almost 100. I have used his little book *'The Apostles' Creed'* (Continuum, 2004 edition) to try and ensure that I do some justice to the mainstream beliefs that the Creed is affirming. It is useful even to me in places, and it does at least include a very quick look at the original historical setting before moving on to an exposition of each phrase.

But it perfectly illustrates the difficulty that so many of us have in engaging in any kind of discussion with people of faith. When looking at the meaning of belief, Cranfield first quotes the German theologian Karl Barth: *'There is no man (sic) who does not have his own god or gods as the object of his highest desire and trust, or as the basis of his deepest loyalty and commitment'*. Fair enough. Few people put their faith in nothing. That's been true since ancient times. But then he gives the game away with what he writes himself. *'The decision that has to be made is not between having a god and not having a god. That choice is not open to us.... The choice to be made is, rather, between believing in the one true living God, the only real God, or believing in one or more of the false gods, behind all of which looms in the background the ultimate idol, each man's or woman's ego.'* (p.9).

This immediately makes me want to give up and run away. Only his 'God' and His ways are real and have nothing to do with bolstering our fragile human egos.

There is no justification offered for such a position; we are just required to accept it. He has discovered the truth; 'God' with a capital G. The rest of us are simply chasing after selfish false trails. We are pursuing only human inventions; he has somehow been able to encounter the only source of actual Divine Reality. But of course that's merely his opinion. He is entitled to it, but not to claim that all others are invalid.

As the quotation from Virgil at the beginning of this book asks, the key issue is 'do the gods create us to fulfil their passions or do we create them to fulfil ours'? He wasn't of course writing in a Christian context, but it's still a very fair question. In what follows I will suggest that we all create our gods to validate our own highest wishes and ideals, not the other way round. That's what religions do, including each version of Christianity. All doctrines, including the specific articles of the Creeds, have to be seen for what they are – attempts by men, (almost entirely by men until very recently), to explain the world around them and to promote their existing human values. They did this by reference to (a) what they already knew to be true at the time and (b) an assumed supernatural basis for what they could not otherwise explain. Gods fill in the gaps.

But what used to be in the second category is now in the first. What was previously a mystery is now explained. There is a rational or scientific reason for how the Universe came into existence, or for day and night, for when it rains or why people get ill and die, or whether you might win or lose a war. A God is not required to make things happen, or not happen. Religions need to catch up with modern reality. Otherwise we can hardly be surprised if most people don't see them as having any value. So do their insights still mean anything at all now that the goalposts have moved so much? Exploring that question is the task I have set myself, even if most 'religious' people don't seem all that bothered. They should be, if they want their beliefs to be taken seriously by anyone else.

All religions are an attempt to understand ourselves, expressed entirely in our own words and activities. A 'religious' experience is only a human experience that we have defined as a religious experience. Have you noticed how often people associate such supposed 'revelations' with emotions, feelings, dreams or physical deprivation? Well maybe they 'just really' wanted to feel that way so they did. Or they are merely dreams or down to physiological changes as a result of a poor diet and a lack of sufficient water. Everything is human. Prayer goes on in our brains and in our thoughts or is expressed through our mouths. The Creeds were created by a no doubt rather tense series of meetings. The Bible was written using historical sources and people's memories. Any sense of the 'Divine' comes through the human; every time and in all cases. There can be no exceptions or we would not be aware of them.

Religious beliefs, like music or art, therefore inevitably reflect their own specific settings, times and places, not all knowledge and experience ever gained or ever to be gained. Many would claim that we have to submit to some kind of external authority in order to understand ourselves. But the idea that my life now can be understood by using only the definitions of those who knew nothing about me is nonsense. I have to do my own work, just as they did, but not necessarily using only the same tools or reaching the same conclusions. Just as Mozart did not know about Vaughan Williams and Turner knew nothing of Picasso, the compilers of the ancient faiths did not know about all the forms of human self-understanding yet to come. Those who have walked this way before us deserve to be studied. But their claims cannot be fixed for all eternity. We now have to express ourselves in new ways because of what has happened since.

If no-one's taking much notice of the Christian perspective any more, and let's face it, very few people are in our Western context, maybe the problem is with the message and the messengers, not with the audience. Much talk, especially of God, no longer speaks our language. The 'truths' that the Creeds traditionally affirm are not necessarily those we need to hear. But life goes on; human experience still presents us with challenges and choices. Is there another way to think that may begin in the same place but which takes us to somewhere different? This may then lead to a new kind of believing; new kinds of 'creeds' in which to place our trust in the modern world.

For me, this still has to be done in response to the Christian story because that's where I belong. I do not want to leave Jesus of Nazareth out of my intellectual or moral landscape. But, just to be clear; I do not consider myself a 'Christian' as most others use the word. I still count myself a fringe member of his community and participate in its Eucharistic life, if only sometimes. But many of the Church's official faith statements, most of which come from long after Jesus himself, are unacceptable to me, especially the idea that he 'died for my sins' as some kind of sacrificial substitute or that any kind of eternal condemnation lies in wait for those who do not believe it.

I hope that I can still keep a slender hold on my heritage, but this is a personal pilgrimage <u>beyond</u> belief as traditionally understood. The 'God' we have created, and the religion Christians have built upon 'Him', both strike me as unhelpful. In that sense, I am, and I am sure I will remain, an atheist and a sceptic. The doctrines I am asked to believe do not answer the questions that I and many others are asking about how to be fully human. Perhaps they even get in the way and make it <u>more</u> difficult to walk in 'the Way' of Jesus. So can there still be a meaningful conversation about all this? Is there any point in still bothering? Many would say not, but the reader is welcome to travel with me for a while. Maybe we can explore these ideas together and discover something new along the way that will encourage us both.

www.ben-whitney.org.uk
November 2019

PART 1

A CREED FOR TODAY?

1   EXPLORING NOT CONFORMING

I have spent my whole life, or at least the last 50-plus years of it, wondering whether there is any truth in the Christian religion into which I was born and raised. I owe an enormous debt of gratitude to my parents for a secure and stable childhood. Church was just taken for granted as an integral part of it. My father was a Baptist Minister, though he became increasingly disillusioned towards the end of his life and, like many others of his generation, eventually found a more purposeful vocation in teaching. My mother, who never had a 'proper' job, was a dutiful Minister's wife until he died and also wrote books of talks for the endless women's meetings that were commonplace in the Free Churches in those days – perhaps they still are. My older brother became a keen evangelical. Christianity is clearly in my genes.

After my father's sudden death in my mid-twenties, I decided to study theology and church history at postgraduate level and then became a Baptist Minister myself, because it seemed the right thing to do at the time. I found my academic studies exciting and stimulating. I learnt to read the New Testament in Greek, as my father had been able to do, (though I've forgotten most of it since!) I discovered great C20th theologians like

Paul Tillich and Dietrich Bonhoeffer. I got involved in the World Council of Churches and its programme of social theology, even spending a short time at the Bossey Institute in Geneva. I came out with a First and added some courses in pastoral ministry and Baptist piety to send me on my way into the 'real' world.

My new church was in a brewery town and this was perhaps the only Baptist Church in the country back then where the deacons took prospective Ministers out for lunch to check that they were not teetotallers! They were generally happy years but I never really managed to reconcile the questions raised by my training with the genuine and sincere faith of the people to whom I was supposed to be ministering week-by-week. In the end I decided that they believed rather more of it all than I did. I always felt a bit at odds with my more enthusiastic 'fraternal' colleagues; (they were virtually all men). So, after a few more years working for the Church of England around the time of 'Faith in the City', and serving as a Lay-Reader in two parishes, I gave up on ministry and on attending any church at all. I'm sure there are other clergy who have similarly 'lost their faith', but who just keep going through the motions, unsure of what it all means to them, but I couldn't do that. My professional career before and since has been in education and social work. I now have no official status in any church; I mostly hang about in the metaphorical porch and only go in every now and then. It's called being 'liminal' apparently, though I didn't know that until recently.

I have only come back to thinking about all this in the last few years. I thought it had all gone away for good but obviously it hadn't. I have written several other short books, which a few people have actually read, and developed a website about 'humanist spirituality' which not many people have looked at. This book is probably my last hurrah. It's been a pretty haphazard journey to here but I have always believed that my life, and the decisions I have made about how to live it, some better than others, are all down to me. I try to respect where others are coming from when they say that God has a 'plan' for them, or a 'purpose' that they should try to follow, but I have never been there. Life brings what it brings. I wouldn't actually want there to be an interventionist God of this kind, though I can see why some may find it a comfort.

Many of the claims of religions make no sense once you stop to analyse them. They may be based on little or nothing that is sustainable once you ask a few simple questions. Many Christians have never done this analysis for themselves. They have put their faith in what they have been told without ever subjecting it to any genuine testing, other than using what 'the Bible says' or their own feelings as 'evidence'. Indeed such unquestioning commitment often seems to be required in order to belong. Certainty still seems popular, at least at the margins of overall decline. I find all this deeply depressing, given our unique human capacity to enquire and evaluate before we commit. Hopefully what I have written here will help others to do that, as well as helping myself to keep exploring.

But my concern is not just about believability. It is also about morality. The debate we need to be having is not only about whether religions are 'true', and what that word actually means. We should also be asking if they are good for us. For centuries religions equalled morality. They showed people how to live well – or they claimed to. In practice, their followers often ignored what they were taught; many of them doing what they thought was right anyway, whatever their priests said. But this often produced a deeply unhealthy cycle of reinforced guilt and conditional forgiveness, underscored by the threat of eventual judgement which, understandably, worked pretty well in keeping the faithful in line, at least nominally. Convince people they have a problem and then tell them that yours is the only solution if they want to avoid everlasting punishment. I never knew I needed a whole range of male grooming products until the good people at L'Oreal told me I was worth it! It's a classic marketing strategy applied to selling 'salvation', but wholly immoral.

Christianity has, of course, been enormously influential on our culture, and therefore on me as an individual. It has brought us many good things and many good people have found a meaning for their lives within it. But its traditional claims don't work now, or not for me and for millions of others like me. As the 2011 UK Census shows, we are gradually embracing a 'secular' world-view, largely as a result of scientific explanations for things that used to be attributed to Divine intervention. In my opinion the First World War dealt the Church a blow from which it has never recovered. How can there be a 'resurrection of the body' when your young son's remains are entirely lost in some muddy Flanders field, never to be returned to you? Indeed, how can there be a 'God' at all?

Twice as many people indicated in 2011 that they had no religion compared to 10 years previously, though most people not allied to any other faith did still tick that they were 'Christian'. But this was largely because of the way the question was worded which assumed you had a nominal religion of some kind unless you specifically opted out. The evidence from the churches themselves suggests something different. Other subsequent more in-depth surveys show that the overwhelming majority of people don't actually believe any of Christianity's teachings or feel any need to worship its God. They're just saying that they are within that particular cultural tradition, or that they identify with that heritage. So do I, though I wouldn't use the C word to describe myself and I wish more people would have the courage of their non-convictions. Even saying that you try to live a 'Christian' life might only be about being a good person, or treating others as you would like to be treated yourself. Actually, that's not a bad standard to live by, according to Jesus anyway.

I don't believe that as a consequence of this loss of religious faith people are necessarily less humane or ethical than they used to be. As will be clear throughout, I don't accept that those who are not Christians have no moral compass or that 'the world' is the antithesis of the way it should be now that the Church has more or less lost its influence. What is different is that just as there are many 'Christianities', there are also many ways of being fully human; many moralities. Since the Enlightenment and the growth of mass education we no longer have to look only to ancient sources or to those who interpret them for our guidance: the sisters are doing it for themselves! In all seriousness, the way in which women have emerged from centuries of repression to bring a new perspective on our life together is a very significant driver of our current context. So much in the past was defined by men, including virtually all our religious language and moral codes. Similarly, we now have insights available to us from those of different cultures, sexualities and ethnicities. Even a child may lead us, though Isaiah knew that long before Greta Thunberg told us what we needed to hear about our planet. As all of these new influences form key elements of our contemporary world-view, can a faith system built almost entirely on patriarchal heterosexual male imagery have any chance of survival without radical rethinking?

If all theology and all religions are contextual; indeed if all human behaviour has to be seen in the light of its setting, does that mean that there is nothing left to believe in? Maybe Virgil and Cranfield were both wrong. We may no longer feel the need to obey Divine commands or to elevate our desires and make them into gods; we just get on with life without giving it much thought. GK Chesterton said that when people stop believing in God, they don't then believe in nothing, they believe in anything. I'm not sure that's fair, but in an era of 'fake news' and when politicians can say that 'truth' is whatever they say it is, some would argue that to avoid such anomie we have to hold on to the Bible, the Creeds and other tried and trusted formulas to stop us drifting about aimlessly. That need for moral authority clearly does still work for some, at least for a while, but not for most.

Our general C21st context is to be suspicious, cautious and no longer obedient or subservient to our 'betters'. That is surely a good thing. They don't deserve it. We are like the little boy who has seen that Emperor has no clothes and are not afraid to say so. If people are to give the God and Jesus story any time at all, we have to tell it in ways that recognise what has changed in the meantime. Otherwise it just becomes irrelevant; something that we may have been told about as children but which we can no longer trust to be true, like Santa Claus. We have a choice. God may have to wait in line; He's not automatically at the front the queue.

But although I am pretty much an outsider looking in at Christianity, I acknowledge that there is also a sense in which I cannot let it go. There are those who would maintain that this is evidence for the 'Hound of Heaven' who will not let go of me! He is still pursuing me, despite my best endeavours to get away. Such an idea of a God who is not really interested in the real me, only in the 'me' He would like me to become, is pretty unattractive and only reinforces my sense that I would want nothing to do with Him even if He were there. It is not that I would like to believe but cannot. To quote Bishop Jack Spong, it's Christianity that must change or it will die. I still want to go on exploring its potential and discovering new ways to make sense of it, but the old ideas will never work for me. It must be possible to do it differently. If not, I'll probably have to give it all up again one day.

My concern is on trying to live well, so it's not surprising that our paths still cross from time to time. But I am no longer convinced (was I ever?) that the traditional formulations of faith show us where we need to go. Perhaps it is time we learned to live without them and found a new kind of faith, primarily in ourselves. We need ever-new 'creeds' for ever-new situations. And ever-new understandings of 'God' as well, or maybe we should just leave the word out of our thinking altogether. We'll see.

* * *

The focus of this book is initially on one of the ancient Creeds or belief-statements that lie at the heart of Christian doctrine but which date from hundreds of years after Jesus himself. They are still based on the New Testament, but they also reflect a very different world as the Church became more organised, powerful and hierarchical, well beyond its original somewhat marginalised context. Some elements of the traditional Creeds are not therefore strictly 'Biblical' but that's exactly what you would expect as human understandings evolve. I just don't think that this process stopped centuries ago as many believers seem to.

What were the Creeds for? Mostly to resolve a specific argument. They were usually hammered out in no-doubt lengthy all-night sessions of (male) representatives from the various Christian communities of the time, primarily across the Mediterranean and Asia Minor. It must have been rather like deciding on a communiqué at the end of an EU summit or an Anglican Synod! The final statements often represented a compromise between different views, or were left ambiguous on purpose so that everyone could assent to them. Some have a very complex background in which a particular assertion is being made deliberately in order to outlaw another. Inevitably they reflect the very different world within which they were created. I do genuinely wonder what people today think they are saying when they repeat them and whether they find any problem reconciling the words with what else they know to be true. I enjoy a beautifully-sung Evensong but when we get to the Creed it feels like there is a massive dissonance between what is assumed to be true for the next two minutes and the way we live the rest of our lives.

The 'Apostles' Creed' was nothing directly to do with the apostles, (the original disciples of Jesus), though there were claims made in antiquity that each of the 12, (presumably not including Judas Iscariot), had contributed a phrase. This has absolutely no validity. Much of the content may reflect older Creeds but, unlike, for example, the 'Nicene' Creed, (which doesn't actually come directly from the Council of Nicaea in 325), the Apostles' Creed cannot be dated to a specific event or time. It is often credited to St Ambrose and the phrase was first used in a letter he wrote about 390. But, according to Professor Cranfield no less, he was probably not referring to all the statements that are now included.

It may not have had the form in which we now know it until around the C8[th] and it is thought to have emerged primarily in the border areas of France and Spain, primarily under the patronage of Charlemagne who died in 814. So that's about as far from the original events that inspired Christianity as we are from the building of Angkor Wat in Cambodia or the exploits of Genghis Khan. Could anything written down now be seen as reflecting accurately what actually happened then? And where else would what was thought to be true over 1200 years ago necessarily still tell us what we need to know today? Of course there are valuable insights to be gained from history. I find much that Confucius is supposed to have written quite helpful, but I wouldn't say he could never be improved upon in the light of further experience.

The Apostles' Creed does not grapple with some of the theological complexities of the other Creeds, including, for example, the exact nature of the relationship between the Holy Spirit, Jesus the Son and God the Father. For this relief, much thanks! These were highly contentious issues then but are entirely lost on us today. Some of the disputes came down, literally, to individual Greek letters. These are such difficult and esoteric arguments, that there is really very little point in getting bogged down in them. I have chosen to explore some of the statements of this particular Creed partly to facilitate my title and partly because it is widely accepted as a summary of the basics, especially across the Western (Roman) tradition. It often forms the basis of vows made at baptism or on entering into a formal commitment of church membership. It is essentially a set of required convictions; not so much designed to settle major disputes this time as to enable those not previously acquainted with Christianity to see what all the fuss was about and to provide agreement about who was 'in', (and, just as importantly, who was not).

Statements of religious faith are not always as explicit as the version I will use in what follows. Creeds are still at the heart of Anglican and Roman Catholic worship, at least in theory. But to participate at all in virtually any church you first have to declare that you have read and will observe the rules – interested enquirers who want to start somewhere else, or bring new truths to bear on what is on offer, are not necessarily welcome. There has, admittedly, been a greater willingness to accept diversity in some areas of Church life, though not everywhere. Many churches would still not accept gays and lesbians as members, for example, or not if there was an open honesty allowed. Even now some believers and official structures still show shocking discrimination against women. This is just prejudice, not a matter of conscience. I don't understand why the Church of England has felt it has to accommodate them by setting up 'alternative oversight'. It wouldn't tolerate a church that wanted to discriminate on grounds of race. Women's ministry has brought massive benefits. I feel sorry for those who have ignored it; they are the losers.

Most churches have chosen, or been forced, to adapt to a greater variety of views about lifestyle, marriage, gender etc. or even fewer people would go just to be told off! Baptism is usually available even if the parents are not married, though not many now take up the offer. There is considerable engagement in local neighbourhoods and charitable work, as well as strictly 'religious' activity, some of it highly commendable, effective and much needed. The association of church with only a certain economic class or ethnic group has weakened significantly. Churches have websites and use social media. There are some experimental faith communities meeting in places that are not church buildings like pubs and people's homes. Adapting to social change has actually been a regular feature of the Church's history. Indeed, without such flexibility it wouldn't have survived as long as it has.

But, in contrast to the USA, for example, where Jack Spong remained a bishop and there are several other radical writers among practising clergy and church leaders, with the exception of the excellent Richard Holloway there seems to be very little open discussion in the UK about the <u>content</u> of Christianity, only its presentation. C of E clergy still have to swear allegiance to the bishop and the 39 Articles. Those who have put their more questioning heads above the parapet have often come to regret it. Look at what happened to John Robinson, Don Cupitt, Anthony Freeman or David Jenkins. Mostly they have been ridiculed, excluded, ignored or have given up in despair. Maybe it's different in mainly academic settings, but no-one seems to notice if so. The relentless onslaught of the Alpha Course has dumbed things down to a list of agreed statements, the very opposite of a genuine search for new ideas that might provide a way in for modern thinking people. Despite what it says on the posters outside, only certain questions are allowed and the 'answers' have all been agreed in advance. Even someone as mainstream as Steve Chalke has been accused of 'heresy' for what seems to be his more universalist interpretation of Paul and rejection of a literal 'hell'.

Some churches pay scant attention to anything that looks like ritual, but nonetheless they have clear doctrinal statements of their own which can be even more prescriptive and exclusive than a Creed. Sometimes the whole thing operates on a series of assumptions about what it means to believe if you want to be part of it. If you doubt this, look at the requirements imposed by most Christian Unions in our universities or check out a few independent church websites. Openness to new ideas is clearly not encouraged. It's all about getting people 'on message'; telling them what they must believe. Reassuring and self-affirming no doubt, but intellectually lazy and often oppressive from where I'm standing.

Although I occasionally attend my local cathedral or a rather inspiring, inclusive and innovative inner-city parish church, I'm not sure that either are entirely typical. Elsewhere I have been made to feel very uncomfortable not only by the general approach and worship style but because the sermon or intercessions assume that I have certain values just because I'm there. Praying for the defeat of any move towards gay marriage or in support of the conversion of the Jews would be two recent examples. How can anyone claim to know the mind of their God in such minute detail? Is it not possible to be a Christian and take another view? Maybe God is happy to leave the gays and the Jews alone while she gets on with other things that are rather more important, like world peace!

These are all examples of the written and unwritten 'creeds' which can be immensely influential, whatever kind of church it is. In contrast to the spirit of enquiry that was prevalent when I was a theology student, it often looks as if believers are expected to have closed minds and clear convictions. They have come to be told 'the' truth. That's what 'having a faith' usually means. It is so often about absolutes; about nailing your colours to the mast. But other kinds of spirituality might look rather different.

Only the Quakers or the Unitarians leave it entirely up to more individual interpretation and have no defined creed to which participants are expected to adhere. I am a member of several 'liberal' Christian groups, though the age profile suggests that they won't be around much longer and few younger people attracted to Christianity seem to want to grapple with the uncertainties involved.

As is already obvious, I have no time at all for those believers whose smug superiority that they alone have grasped the truth seems to greatly outweigh their compassion and common humanity. Thankfully such an approach will only ever appeal to a small minority in an open-minded society like ours. The rest of us are happy to be on the outside. Saying something from a great height or in a loud voice does not necessarily make it right. Religions have often got things wrong. This is only to be expected given that we have created them all. But, in my opinion, all religions' inherent weaknesses should make believers act and speak with some caution, especially when it comes to questions of morality. I and many others find it increasingly difficult to take lectures on how we should live from those whose beliefs often seem to lead them to values that promote human unhappiness and a frequently exclusive judgementalism.

Conventional creeds seek to define the boundaries and keep everyone in line. They rarely seem to set people free. My quest is not for any kind of replacement experience of that kind. I may be looking for a new understanding of believing, but I do not seek a new kind of 'religion' to go with it. The Credal statements are supposed to encapsulate the very essence of faith, but they seem to be as much about 'assent' as 'faith; just asking us to agree to certain things, not really explaining why we should do so. So you say you 'believe' in God? Is that only about the fact that you believe 'He' exists? Or is it about what difference it makes to your life? Let's focus on that instead.

Karen Armstrong in her book '*St Paul: The Misunderstood Apostle*' (Atlantic Books, 2015), argues that the NT Greek word *pistis*, usually translated as 'belief' or 'faith', actually means 'have loyalty to', deliberately linked to the contrasting oath to the Emperor that was originally required. It's not about maintaining a collective conformity but about what I personally trust in and am committed to living by. A commitment to a particular way of life has to have real substance, not just be based on a set of familiar clichés that we keep repeating because that's what we have always done and we don't like the thought of the alternative. But what do the statements actually mean for day-to-day living, and is the meaning the same now as it was 500, 1500 or 2000 years ago? That's what I try to explore, in different ways, in both Parts 1 and 2 of what follows.

This is not 'faith seeking understanding', (St. Anselm 1033-1109). That implies that a given belief is the starting point and then we have to find a way to make sense of it in the 'real' world. If anything it is the opposite. I start from 'facts seeking faith': 'This is what I and others know to be true in my rational human experience. Can I find a way of relating the Christian tradition to it'? It has to be that way round. For now I am happy to go on trying to explore the particular story about life that comes to me through Jesus of Nazareth, and only occasionally looking to other religious or philosophical traditions that are less familiar to me. In that sense, this is still a search for a form of humanist 'Christianity', if not as the word is usually understood.

It is a huge mistake to see a religion as doing all the work for you. The question Jesus apparently asked his disciples was 'Who do you say I am'?, not 'Here's who others tell you I am or what it says about me in a book or a list of statements with which you are required to agree if you want to be involved'. I am a genuine partner in this process of discovery, not merely lost in ignorance until I am shown 'the' way. I cannot alter the facts about the modern world as I understand them, or change how I believe it is right to live, in order to fit in with a predetermined set of requirements. It has to be the other way round. Life as I know it is the starting point; the choices involved in being human are where we must begin. Any faith then follows – if it works. That's actually the way it's always been.

The Apostles' Creed therefore provides my historical starting-point even though I can't affirm most of what it says. But I want to use some of what it claims to ask if we can now make new 'spiritual' definitions based entirely on a non-'religious' understanding of ourselves. In effect, a 'humanist creed', but growing from the same Christian roots. The aim is to go beyond my lack of faith in 'Christianity' in order to discover something that actually relates to the modern world; a living thing, not a dying one. I hope that at least some of Jesus' followers will share the journey with me. I may be an apostate, but I still have a value system and a moral commitment to the good of humanity. Most people do. Like everything else we believe and experience, this too does not come from outside of ourselves but is part of ourselves. So is there anything in these ancient understandings that can still help me? Perhaps there are insightful truths behind the assertions, or new truths are now available, unknown to those that went before, that we can now rely on instead. Perhaps these can still form a framework for a system of belief, even after the specific doctrines have been found to have feet of clay.

But why did the ancient writers assert what they did? Is there any value in still following their direction of travel? What can I believe in? I do not believe the traditional statements as they stand, nor do I believe in them as the only way forward in deciding how best to live. They belong in the past. But they may still offer me some pointers to help illuminate the present. It looks like there is some useful work to be done if I am to reach any kind of destination, so let's get on!

2 INFINITE POSSIBILITIES

'I believe in God, the Father Almighty, Creator of heaven and earth.'

The Apostles' Creed begins, of course, with a God, as (virtually) all religions do, almost by definition. Most civilisations throughout recorded human history have believed in and worshipped gods of some kind; from the celestial projections of the ancient Egyptians, Romans and Greeks, to the spirit worlds and polytheisms of many Eastern and African belief systems and the shared convictions of the 'People of the Book': Jews, Christians and Moslems. The human need to find a meaning outside of ourselves which explains the way things are appears to be almost universal – at least until relatively recently. It may seem rather self-opinionated to suggest they got it wrong. For many this ends the argument about 'a' God behind it all, but just saying so is no longer convincing.

The quest for a God begins, as it must do, with us. Religions always fit their cultural context; they make sense sociologically. The believers began with what they knew. People probably first worshipped the moon and the sun or at least had a sense that what they could see in the heavens was much bigger than they were and was therefore worthy of their submission. Gods had to be appeased and given what it was thought they wanted in order to avoid future disaster. The physical world seemed an awesome and frightening place; even more so when we had little or no control over its excesses of climate, disease and natural phenomena. Most of all, death is inevitable. The human individual can obviously feel somewhat insignificant by comparison and religions met the desire for order, meaning and structure. Hence the need for a Creator, or even a whole army of them.

To me, in my time, the beauty of the natural world, like the heavens, declares the glory only of itself, not of a Creator. It no more needs a supernatural explanation to make it worthy of admiration and value than does a Rachmaninov piano concerto. That would not have been enough for most of those who lived before me. But these 'religious' interpretations are still all <u>our</u> insights, not a discovery of a pre-existing truth 'out there'. It's obvious when you think about it.

Think through with me a couple of early examples from within the Judao/Christian tradition. Any claim that a God created the world in 7 'days' requires a system of days to be <u>already</u> present before such an idea can be taught or believed as the way that a God works. The days were a neutral context provided by the Universe, then given an additional meaning as part of the human understanding of our solar system and the development of a specific Jewish cycle of work and rest. Other civilisations created other cycles, other 'weeks' and other gods; just as the Egyptians created a god that they thought controlled the Nile. But it flooded just as part of the way the world was. It's all to do with astronomy, geography and climate. Gods don't make things happen; they are a language to explain what happens anyway.

Genesis Chapter 1, (or Chapter 2 which is older), are clearly not scientific factual accounts of the way things first came about. Given that there was no sun until day 4, 'days' 1-3, as we understand the word, could not have existed. The story 'proves' nothing. The ancient writers already had days to use as a metaphor for creation over time, so they used this to hang their beliefs upon. They may even have been using 'day' in the same sense as the text that talks about a day being 'like' a thousand years from their God's perspective, never intending it to be taken 'literally'. So they devised a creation myth that fitted in with what they already knew, (or, more likely, borrowed it from elsewhere and adapted it). 'Our world is like this and its deeper significance for us is this'; not 'this is what was previously true before us so this is what we therefore have to believe'.

The ancient myths of Adam and Eve and their descendants are the same. They reflect the already-existing reality that human beings had the unique power to make moral choices; the threat from natural predators, competition for scarce land, conflict between tribes etc. Just as previous civilisations had done, the ancient Jewish writers then transferred these elements of the human community onto the cosmos. They came up with different answers; not for them a set of capricious deities but One Creator directing it all for a greater purpose. But the process is exactly the same as before. The compilers of the historic faiths just could not conceive of a value for their own existence other than as a result of the action of some higher Power beyond themselves. 'What are we?' asked the Psalmist. Well, in truth, not much; but that's not a very happy thought. So they devised an explanation. Their personal value came from being part of a Divine plan. Humankind cannot have created itself and built its own world to live in; so how else could it all have come about other than through the direct activity of an over-arching, pre-existing God?

Well now we know how it all happened; or we have a pretty good set of theories that go a long way to providing solutions to these age-old questions that were not available before. A God, or a whole collection of them, is/are not necessarily required. Maybe the Universe just is. It doesn't have an explanation of this kind. We are just on our own and have to <u>make</u> some sense of it all. We might like the idea of a 'first cause' or a deeper purpose but perhaps it all happened for no underlying reason, long long before all gods, religions and the human beings who created them. Can there be a Creator who was not Himself created? What created God? Aren't we still left with something from nothing? A spontaneous God is on offer; so why not a spontaneous Universe instead?

Many people find this idea of creation from nothing difficult to accept. A scientist friend of mine who is also a Christian says it makes no sense from within his perspective where everything has a relationship to everything else. If the physical world contains explanations, causes and effects within it for the way things are, how can its own existence have no cause, no explanation? My response is that it does have an explanation; it was created from nothing – like me. I did not exist until I was conceived and born. You can trace the mechanics of my existence back to the actions of my parents but you won't find 'me' waiting there! The potential existed, but not the reality. I came into existence from nothing; I did not exist before; I will not exist again one day. Only the conditions that enabled me to come into existence were already there, then I arrived from nowhere. Like the Universe. QED- sort of!

Arguing otherwise leaves me with so many other unanswered questions. Religion in any form, as it belongs only within the later stages of the human story, is just a few thousand years old. The Universe is staggeringly old by comparison. I have walked on basalt columns at the Giant's Causeway in Northern Ireland that are at least 60,000,000 years old, possibly older. The Earth is probably about 4,500,000,000 years old; the whole known Universe has been around for about 14,000,000,000 years. If the age of the Universe is the height of a room, human beings wouldn't even reach the top of the underlay beneath the carpet.

What was the One God doing during all those noughts if His primary focus is us? What was the point of all those millions of centuries that came before us? And much much more than our Earth is involved. We are just a tiny part of 'the heavens' ourselves not separate from them. We can no longer look only outwards from earth. Now we can also see it from the outside we know how tiny we are. It's thought that there are many as 17,000,000,000 planets that are much the same size as ours, just in our galaxy, let alone what there might be in others.

Perhaps we are just the latest in a long line of Divine projects that have also kept God busy in countless other Universes of which we are unaware. If so, why should such a big God be so involved in such a minor enterprise as our human history, which hardly scratches the surface of time, when He has all the rest at His disposal? Or, if we are unique in getting His attention, why us? Why here? An eternal God who, after aeons of doing nothing, suddenly became especially interested in planet Earth and its inhabitants, just seems one impossibility too many. Conventional Christian faith assumes that the whole of creation was designed for the purpose of a God to reveal Himself to us in His Son in this particular corner of it billions of years later. (We'll come back to some other questions arising from this idea in Chapters 3 and 4). To me that suggests a much more over-inflated idea of our own importance than merely asking whether we may have got it wrong before.

No doubt many would say it's all a mystery and we're not supposed to understand it. After all, we are talking about God here, or trying to, and the size of it all suggests there is much more to it than we can possibly know. But a God, or gods, behind everything is only one possible explanation, albeit a rather attractive one to some people – as long as it's your God that turns out to be the right one. Isn't it strange how human communities always seem to have encountered the gods that favoured them in particular? Yahweh is all for the Jews, Jesus for the Christians and Allah for the Moslems. They each see it as being chosen. Isn't it rather more likely that they have done the choosing? And that, of course, is a key part of the problem. These theories about very different gods that are always on our side cannot <u>all</u> be right, even if there were actually only one God behind everything.

Each human spiritual tradition believes that it has got to the heart of the matter, but they don't all come to the same conclusions, even within the same religion. There is a wide variety of personalities to choose from: gods that enter into the full riches of human sexuality to gods that seem to regard the whole idea as a terrible uncontrollable mistake. Gods that are constantly intervening to influence what goes on, to gods who are utterly indifferent or above human comprehension. How can I possibly know which one to believe in? If you are to accept any god as the explanation for the way things are, don't you also have to reject the claims of those who make other irreconcilable claims about him/her/them? So do you simply choose the 'God' that makes most sense or that you like the sound of? Or are you effectively stuck with the one that happened to hold sway in the culture and community into which you were born?

The overwhelming majority of believers stay within their inherited tradition. If I had been born elsewhere perhaps I would now be trying to have this debate in the context of an entirely different religion. I never chose Western Christianity as my starting point; I was just given it. How handy that it turned out to be the right one! That sounds like the ultimate postcode lottery. Maybe, it could be argued, there are many paths up the same mountain and so on. But can there possibly be more than one true understanding of the one true God, all of which are equally valid, no matter what they each claim to know about Him and however much they vary from one another? It makes no sense to many modern minds.

This is not merely a semantic debate. The existence of a 'God' is where we have to start, but it is not the end of the matter. Some understandings of God, even if 'He' did exist, are utterly unacceptable to me. If the God of the Christians is also the God who took delight in the slaughter of whole tribes and nations in Old Testament times, or the God of the Nazis, the apartheid regime and the conquistadors, then you can most certainly keep Him. He's just pretending to love us in Jesus if He is also capable of sanctioning such cruelty. 'Him', of course, is a loaded concept before we even start. How odd that the one God really is a perfect fit with the patriarchal Jewish, Christian and Islamic communities who worship Him! His Fatherhood is just like ours, only better. At least more polytheistic religions found room for a wider variety of deities. But it's patently clear where all these ideas come from – us. Our ideas of what we mean by 'God' are a reflection of what we know; they always have been.

Perhaps God evolves. He's not as cruel as He used to be, at least in the modern C of E version. But now we really are in the realms of nonsense. Surely it's only the human ideas that have evolved? Our understanding of ourselves no longer needs to seek the reassurance of a tribal god who will put us first. It is time to revisit the idea of a God that we created in the first place. Beliefs have often been revised, but at least let's be honest about it and admit what we are doing. Like Dostoyevsky's Ivan Karamazov, I would even say that we have to do so. It is a moral imperative to rid ourselves of previous outdated ideas and find a new moral basis to our lives that is more in tune with the world as we now understand it. The old God simply has to go.

The compilers of the Creeds had no such worries. Theirs was a three-decker Universe and that was that: a flat earth with God up in heaven above. What was below was a matter of some debate in Jesus' time, but you wouldn't want to go there! It had crystallised into at least some form by the C8th, though many of the claims that believers often take for granted, (even if they don't really believe them), are later even than this, not part of the original Christian package at all. If, as we now know, the spatial concepts are all wrong, then perhaps the theological ideas behind them are too. But it really matters. If there is no God, 'up there' or anywhere else, then no redemption of the gulf between us is required. No redemption, then no Son of God is needed to make it happen, and so on. If there is to be any hope for a better world, it must be found elsewhere; this God story is not the heart of it. This is the key issue that Theists seem to have difficult grasping. They keep talking to us as if we are still living in the 8th (or the 1st) Century.

The whole doctrinal edifice falls if there is no God of the kind they thought then, or if the claims for 'His' existence are no longer intellectually or morally convincing. We have found a freedom to work it out for ourselves that makes conventional religion irrelevant. We are not likely to 'come to church' if we think the whole thing is founded on a mistake. There are other kinds of social clubs on offer if that's all we want. We won't see why we need to accept Jesus as our 'Saviour' if we don't believe we have

~26~

any need to be 'saved', just because there is claimed to be a God who will be angry with us if we're not; (or who loves us and wants us to love Him – take your pick). There is no point in singing hymns or praying to a God who is <u>not there</u> to hear us. It's the supposed reality of a God that no longer means anything; it's not just a selfish desire to stay in bed, wash the car or go shopping on a Sunday morning instead.

So, I have a question for those who still maintain God's existence, and not just as an idea but as a reality. None of the traditional 'proofs' actually prove anything. But that's where your Creed starts. Go on then; convince me! Why should I believe it? Is there anything more to it than just what you say? I hear plenty of self-authenticating talk about a God, but I am none the wiser about why you are so sure that He is the 'answer', no matter how certain you sound. As I argued in the previous Chapter, the true test of any belief is in what difference it makes to <u>life</u>. The track record of religions and the reality of many contemporary churches are both frankly unimpressive when it comes to demonstrating that a God is in charge. The church is so clearly a human organisation, just like any other. Quoting the Bible as the source of it all, or just your own feelings, hardly ends the discussion. The counter arguments are rarely explored, or they are just set up as an 'Aunt Sally' to be knocked down again.

My guess is that <u>genuine obstacles</u> to there being an actual God <u>aren't taken seriously</u> because of a fear there might be some truth in them. We just don't talk about it with any degree of openness. The debate might upset the faithful and, perish the thought, it might even make them question whether they really believe it either. So let's pretend there isn't an issue. But maybe the elephant in the room is that there is no elephant! I am asked simply to take the existence of a God as a matter of 'faith', but outside my normal processes of decision-making and human experience. Religious people really do not seem to understand that many of us cannot do that anymore.

All I see is human beings believing what they choose to believe and telling me I should do the same. If there is a God, much religion entirely fails to make 'Him' real. This is not about asking for allegedly supernatural inexplicable events that will blow our socks off. I can get that by watching Dynamo! That approach used to work in the past: so much was unexplained that a God could be used to fill in all the gaps. It was a God (or gods) who grew (or destroyed) the crops, cured (or sent) diseases and who controlled the future. No it wasn't. We know now that the world doesn't operate according to a Divine whim like that. That interventionist God is dead.

So what's left? 'God' can only ever be a metaphor or a simile for something greater than our individual selves. We can call the Universe 'God', or say love is 'God', or talk of an unknowable mystery. We can think of 'God' as 'being itself', or as an underlying force, not as 'a' Being. Or we can drop the word altogether. But all I can ever know about this supposed God must always be found within my human experience; and that takes me no further than Jesus, an actual human person who I can choose to follow. That is as much of a 'God' as I can conceive of. The rest is all speculation.

I cannot start my own creed with a God as traditionally understood. I have to start with us, as religion has actually always done, but also with what Jesus seems have said about us. More of that later. But, Theist, let's at least talk about our shared humanity. Show me what really matters to your God in the real world. Actually, rather than talk so much, listen. Because I exist. That I know. There may well be 'spiritual' truths to be discovered, but they have to be found within the human condition, not outside of it. It's not asking me to have an inexplicable and irrational faith in something impossible that will get me interested. It's whether or not what you call 'God' can be a new dimension to my current reality. It's a bit like the irritating way that whenever I ask someone to help me with a computer problem they either do it for me or just tell me things I don't understand. I want them to show me and to do it with me. Just telling us there's a God doesn't help. Maybe what you attribute to a God I can still affirm as true even if it comes from us – like the importance of caring for one another or the need for forgiveness when we make mistakes. 'Worshipping' is not my priority; living well – being fully human – is.

Faith has traditionally been about asking people to adopt an alternative world-view from the one that we see day-to-day. That used to work when life was essentially nasty, brutish and short and people felt entirely unable to influence what happened. Of course, like everyone else, I sometimes despair at the state of things. But, guess what? Life can be good! Human beings are frequently magnificent, not 'miserable offenders' who are fundamentally flawed in everything they do. And when things do go wrong, it's clearly down to us to sort it out, and we can. Of course we don't get everything right. Later Chapters will have to address that. But we are not a total disaster. We can love, laugh and be kind and generous to one another. We have conquered so much that used to bind us. We do not need to be told every week that we are hopeless sinners who cannot cope alone. We can be happy with ourselves and live life to the full. Millions do.

Being human in the C21st is an awesome responsibility, worthy of our respect and reverence. We can build enormously powerful weapons to kill each other or we can use the same technology to create new sources of energy that can sustain the world. We can carry out holocausts, pogroms and genocides or we can harness our knowledge and skill to eradicate illnesses and enable children to be born without life-limiting inherited conditions. We can feed and pamper ourselves to excess or we can share the world's resources more equitably. We can probably even destroy the very planet that gave birth to us, or act together to save it. 'Now I am become Death, the destroyer of worlds' said Robert Oppenheimer, quoting the Hindu scriptures, after the Trinity nuclear weapons test in July 1945, (there's an ironic name for it). Or we can choose Life instead, and focus our energies on creativity. We have indeed become gods, but it doesn't have to be in a bad way. I don't see that potential as wrong, idolatrous or sinful. It's a simple fact. We have discovered so much that we used to attribute to a God. Only we can make the difference; there is no God to do it for us.

We can seek a deeper dimension to what it means to be human while we have the chance, or we can waste it all. We have the ability to create something better, or to mess it up. Even if there is no God, there is always a need to <u>live up to my full potential</u> and to find a deeper and more wholesome humanity. Let's talk about all that as our shared human destiny rather than asking me to focus on an external Deity that I just don't believe is there. We can be what we used to think only God could be. We can make the world a better place and discover our true selves in the process. We can make all things new, if we choose to. The possibilities are limitless. 'God', as Anthony Freeman so rightly observed, even though he got no thanks for it, is in us. This much I believe.

Religion emerged from societies as a way of finding order + meaning = a language to explain life - creation myth

Order/divine plan → reassuring

Religion 7000 yrs old, universe 4½ billion years

God you get born into & which you choose

↓ stay with the God you inherit

God is a reflection of what we know

Idea of God can evolve

God - concept was added to

What difference does God make

God as an interventionist

God - a metaphor for something beyond our comprehension

God must exist within our experience

We have discovered

3   AN UNHOLY ALLIANCE

'I believe.... in Jesus Christ his only Son, our Lord,
who was conceived by the power of the Holy Spirit
and born of the Virgin Mary..'.

The doctrines of the Incarnation and the Trinity have
never made much sense to me, nor, I suspect, to many
who still identify themselves as Christians. God is our
Father but He is also his own Son, and He exists as a
Spirit. Jesus was a real human being who died just like
we do; but, absolutely uniquely, he came back from the
dead and is still alive somewhere else now. Indeed, the
Son always existed as a part of God from the beginning of
time, long before there was a man from Nazareth called
Jeshua benJoseph, (a more accurate rendering of the
Hebrew/Aramaic. 'Jesus' is an English word translated
from the Greek).

The Holy Spirit is God too, but is not the Father or the
Son as well. God is One, but also three. That's the official
view but who actually understands it? Not me for sure. I
always used to explain the Trinity as being like molecules
of H2O which can appear as water, steam and ice but
apparently that is not 'sound'. The image of one family
comprising different individuals is sometimes used but

does that make God a kind of committee? I'm sure there is supposed to be rather more to it than that but maybe it's a start. That's the image shown in Rublev's famous icon. 'God' is a community, not an individual. But that still doesn't work for me, other than as poetry or art. Maybe that's all we can ever say, but the Church has made much more of it than that.

There is some evidence to suggest that those who wrote the Creeds found it just as much of a struggle to be clear about what they meant. The meetings went on for years! Did they really need to bother? The Trinity is a very late doctrine, and, perhaps surprisingly, you won't find the actual word in the Bible at all. It was essentially designed to outlaw the Arian 'heresy' which said that Jesus was himself created and was therefore less than God, though I'm pretty sure that is exactly what Paul believed. Yesterday's orthodoxy can easily become tomorrow's heresy. A God who makes Himself known in three different ways was not considered to be enough, though that idea is at least understandable. What they ended up with was a God who is in three persons, (though perhaps 'personalities' is a better translation), but there is still only one God. I have occasionally heard massively complex sermons on all this and at least tried to read some pretty complicated books, but I confess I am none the wiser. How many people in churches on a Sunday, I wonder, have the first idea what they are affirming at this point? Perhaps the concept never was believable, so of course we can't make it so today.

Much of the difficulty comes from the idea that a God can have a 'Son'. I know what a son is; I was one and I have one. Once you start to say that God has a Son in the same sense as we do, you end up tying yourself into all kinds of knots. The image, quite clearly, is another example of how beliefs about God are all metaphors and similes driven by the human understandings and experiences that were there already. We don't know what the word 'son' means because God had one first to show us. We know what the word means from our here and now lives, and <u>then</u> we have tried to make the relationship between God and Jesus a bit like the father/son relationship we already have. But it doesn't really stand up. Or at least we should never see it as anything more than a picture or a story, not a statement of literal, and certainly not biological or physical, fact.

The whole concept is obviously heavily influenced by its social context – not least the repeated emphasis on maleness, reflecting the societies that devised these beliefs and the importance of sons within them. Can you even imagine that God might have had a baby girl at Bethlehem when She wanted to save the world? Or that the Trinity could have been as much 'Mother, Daughter and Holy Spirit' as the usual way of expressing it? Jesus was male; but the eternal 'Word', that he is supposed to be as well, cannot be. A God cannot be male as we understand the word and no-one should find such a statement in any way controversial. If you do, haven't you simply fallen into an entirely human cultural stereotype? An even more bizarre addition is the title sometimes given to Mary as the 'Mother of God'. This is another claim that cannot possibly be true and it contradicts every other statement about the pre-existing Unity within the Trinity. She may have given birth to Jesus; she cannot possibly have given birth to God.

There are some 'givens' before we start. Jesus of Nazareth, whose existence I am happy to affirm, was a real human being, not just masquerading as one. This was another early heresy that the Creeds were designed to reject. It is not enough to say that he 'appeared in human form'. He was as human as I am. It is also a distortion to believe that he was some kind of superman who didn't feel pain, who had magic powers, knew the future and had no faults or weaknesses, though I suspect it is very common to see him in that way. The suggestion that he alone was 'begotten, not made' or was 'without sin' is therefore untenable. If so, he wasn't human. Saying that he was genuinely human also means that he was mortal: made in the same way as we are; born to die, just like everyone else.

If Jesus was actually some other kind of Being temporarily 'sent' from elsewhere – the second person of a Trinity, who had existed as part of God since the very beginning and who only became a human being for a while – then we are effectively talking about two Jesuses – one human and finite and one Divine and eternal. John seems to be wrestling with a similar idea at the beginning of his gospel. But if this cosmic Jesus/Word is an integral part of God, was the committee one down while he was on Earth? Where was Jesus for the billions of years before he 'became' a human being? Where is he now? 'With God' does not answer the question, it only adds to the difficulty. If he had to be born like me to get here, how did he get back again? This might all sound rather flippant but the idea has to mean something if we are to be expected to believe it.

And, of course, we have to find a way of explaining <u>how</u> God could have had a Son if we are to see the idea as a statement of biological fact. Gods do not have children; or rather, the monotheistic Jewish tradition was created in deliberate contrast to other gods on offer at the time who allegedly sired children all over the place. Their God was never meant to be like them. The gospel narratives in Matthew and Luke did their best to fill in the gaps, long after the event, but they really don't add up and they are not even consistent with each other.

Much of the later tradition is based on a mistranslation of the Old Testament text in Isaiah about a 'virgin' bearing a son who would be called 'Emmanuel' or 'God with us'. It's almost mainstream now to accept that this never meant a child born without sex or who uniquely shared God's own nature. In a late Greek version of the Hebrew scriptures, the specific term *'parthenos'* was chosen to render a word that just means 'young woman' in the original. This translation was then used for the versions of what we call the Old Testament that the gospel writers had available. Some contemporary Bibles even show this, at least in the margin. And, of course, it wasn't actually written about Jesus in the first place but about an unspecified coming Messiah.

Just as importantly, a woman made pregnant by a Divine Spirit does not produce a human being. At this time, and for centuries afterwards, women were believed to play no active part in reproduction. They were just a vessel for the baby created entirely by the man's seed. A child, who was believed to have had no genes or DNA inherited from <u>any</u> human person, (and that is the

'Biblical' claim at this point if you take it literally), would not be human. This is the stuff of science fiction or at least of mythology, not real history. Like all religious language it cannot be taken at face value.

It doesn't even work as a theological or literary device. If Joseph was not Jesus' father then Jesus of Nazareth was not really of the 'house and lineage of David' or 'born of Jesse's line' as he has to be in order to be recognised as the Messiah. That's the whole point of the events (which are impossible to date to the same time as each other) that supposedly led to him being born in Bethlehem as predicted, even though the family actually lived in Nazareth. And then you then have to invent a kind of back story about how Joseph came to be seen as his father, even though he wasn't. But if he is not, there is an inherent contradiction at the heart of the nativity stories which entirely undermines the fulfilment of the ancient prophesies that they are trying to demonstrate.

Let's face it; the churches might be fuller than usual at Christmas but few people really believe it all or even understand what it is that they are singing about. It's a nice story, (except for the Herod bit which isn't usually mentioned). But quite a lot of it: stable, innkeeper, donkey, cattle (lowing or otherwise), 'kings', snow, holly, ivy etc. isn't actually there in any of the gospels. But how can it possibly be literally true? It's an atmosphere to embrace, not a blunt instrument to hit the faithless over the head with. Like the whole idea of a God, we are usually asked just to accept all this, not to try and analyse it. But that really won't do.

We created all this complex theory about a pre-existent Son of God who required a one-off suspension of all natural processes in order to be 'born' as a man. So why must we always be stuck with it? It's time to start again. The Church got along very well without Christmas for centuries until the mid-winter Roman festival of Saturnalia provided a useful peg to hang it on. The first Christians, who didn't even have the gospels to read, knew nothing of these stories. They weren't important to who Jesus was for them. A miraculous birth was not initially required, so why would it be difficult to let it go?

It seems very likely that Jesus had no sense of 'Sonship' until his baptism by John the Baptist. This was when he began to speak publically about his mission to change and challenge the Jews. Perhaps he should even be seen as an apostate! His was certainly a radical reinterpretation of his inherited faith which its leaders saw as blasphemous. As Mark, the earliest gospel writer, says, his baptism seems to be when Jesus started to see himself as having some kind of greater purpose in line with the previous 'sons of God' (with a small 's') who are a frequent occurrence in the Old Testament, not a unique creation. The kings had this title, among others. Sons of God were begotten after their birth, not before, (e.g. Psalm 2 v.7). Jesus saw himself as a servant of his God; a messenger, a teacher, a prophet, but in no way on a par with Him. This all strikes me as much more understandable, even if I don't believe in a God Being in the same way. Jesus never claimed to 'be' God. (John's gospel has clearly put his own words into Jesus' mouth. They cannot possibly be his speeches, spoken in Greek, remembered *verbatim*).

I have much less to say at this point about the idea of a 'Holy Spirit' – another dimension of God, still with us after Jesus had gone back home. So not with us before then? Or is God always best thought of as a Spirit? Again, the gospels and the book of Acts are inconsistent. The Old Testament suggests that this Divine Spirit had always been active in the world. Luke's version of the Day of Pentecost says that it came weeks after the resurrection; while John says it was all part of the Easter experience. Turning this belief into a 'person' alongside the Father and Son creates a specifically Christian idea that cannot be reconciled with what went before, when the One 'God' was just 'God' who could not be known. It may have more to do with identifying the Jesus movement as different from the Jews than with anything actually about 'God'. Or the first Christians needed a 'Comforter'. Again, these are human ideas raised up to the heavens, not the other way round.

Bishop Jack Spong (quoting Paul) talks of Jesus having a 'spirit of holiness' which is why we still bother with him. I find that more helpful. He is the exemplar of a spiritual dimension to human life, not a unique 'person' within a Godhead. That only came in much later. We again need metaphors to express this sense of the 'spiritual'; a wind, an energy, a breath; perhaps life itself. It is good to seek it out, but as an element of our shared humanity, not as something from outside of ourselves. It is universal among us and it blows wherever it wills. It unlocks our potential, sustains the world and all those who dwell in it according to the ancient chroniclers and prophets, not just a minority of enthusiastic Christians.

This whole concept has sometimes been hijacked by those who have turned the Spirit (with a capital S) into something that only a privileged few have encountered. There has been a fashion to make a lot of it in recent years, though it seems to be waning a little again now. Those who make such confident claims are just experiencing a psychological state that they choose to see in this way. It's a human experience like any other, whatever you call it. Tying it up in a doctrine of the Trinity, or making this spiritual dimension to life the exclusive possession of only some, entirely misses the point that the original writers were making about both Jesus and the post-Jesus experience. (See also Pentecost Sunday in Part 2).

But why did the Trinity come to matter so much? Edward Wightman (a Baptist from the same town where I used to be a Minister!) was the last man burnt at the stake in England, in Lichfield marketplace in April 1612, primarily for denying it. Judging by the contemporary accounts he was clearly far from a well man, though it may have been the torture that caused his final delusions. But, incredibly, it was illegal not to believe in it, or at least to say so out loud, until 1813! What was the reason for being expected to believe in a three-dimensional God like this? It became so important because of what Jesus was subsequently believed to have done by dying. He was a sacrifice, they thought, picking up from a familiar image in the Old Testament. Religious piety at that time was widely based on the concept of something, usually an animal, being required to appease or satisfy God. For conventional Christian faith it has to be God who did it all, not just a man being sacrificed. Jesus has to be God too or he would be the unjustly-treated victim of a tyrant. Which brings us to the real point of both the Incarnation and the Trinity. And the reason why we don't still need them.

The initial Christian context, before the Trinitarian theology was devised, was in people's sense of their vulnerability and transience. This was the human problem to be solved. Life was hard. Yes we have enormous possibilities for greatness, but we also live with tragedy, loss and inhumanity. Death stalked society back then in a way that we can scarcely comprehend today unless you live in places like Iran, Afghanistan or Syria. Jesus was not a young man if he lived to 33; that was greater than the average life-expectancy. The dead and dying were everywhere, not least when nations were under brutal occupation or if you faced persecution. This is the backdrop to the first believers in New Testament times. So they created a theology about a God which offered them a hope of 'salvation' and something better to come. No wonder at least some people embraced it. I can entirely understand that.

But when the Church became powerful by the C4th, and then well into the time of the Apostles' Creed and even up to the present day, it needed a stronger hold over the faithful. It was the master now. So the Trinitarian 'God' became the source of their authority who kept His servants in a state of grateful dependency. The reason why God was believed to have had a Son, revealed and created through His Spirit, both of whom were also a part of Himself, was supposedly all wrapped up in making 'atonement' happen. It put things right between us and Him and, in the process, just happened to bolster the importance of His official representatives on earth who decided who could benefit, and therefore who couldn't. What power they now wielded! Life, death, heaven, hell, everything. To me this all smacks of what was wrong with religion before Jesus, not how it should have been afterwards. I don't believe he has had anything at all to do with it.

These are big Christian ideas which are probably lost on many of those who are still turning up on Sundays much more often than I do. But believing in a Trinitarian God is not just about a cosy feeling that He is with you to help you through life's many difficulties. It's not even that Jesus provides you with some comfort that he has been there too or that there is a Divine Spirt to sustain us. It's that without all this you're toast! There is no hope without it. God in Jesus has healed an otherwise permanent wound in the human condition, called 'original sin' by Augustine. An inherited fracture between us and the Divine Being who made it all. But we have the answer you need! Those who write the Creeds control the outcomes, as they still do. I am tempted to say that if this isn't what you think it's all about, then you're probably no more a 'proper' Christian than I am. Welcome!

I'll come back in Chapter 4 to the whole issue of how we can understand Jesus' death in entirely rational terms. But granted that I can't believe that this whole cosmology of multiple Godheads is real, can I at least identify with the problem it was designed to solve? The hope has to be found within our human experience, not beyond it. Not, for me, a broken relationship with a God, but certainly a broken relationship with one another. We need to go back again to the very beginning of the story. The insight of the ancient writers of the early Chapters of Genesis was that human relationships, and our relationship to the physical Earth, were both less wholesome than they could be. Life was a struggle and the human community often turned upon itself; man against woman; brother against brother; farmer against farmer; nation against nation. That still rings true.

The story begins with Adam and Eve, Cain and Abel etc., (obviously not actual individual people but representative stereotypes). These ancient myths, like the Tower of Babel, are all about us falling out with each other and failing to look after our world properly. The fractured relationship with God comes in as the explanation for why things were as they were, given that a religious understanding was about the only one on offer in pre-scientific times. But I want to stop before that point. To recognise the problem but also to affirm the importance of what we can be at our best, not only of what has gone wrong. If we still need an atonement, (an at-one-ment) it is between us and other people, not with a God.

Nearly everyone would say that they derive their greatest happiness from their families. That's where we give and receive love, for the mutual benefit of all. If an example of 'Sonship' is at the heart of it, then perhaps we need to begin by affirming the significance of our own closest relationships. Family life isn't always all it's cracked up to be, but this was the nearest analogy that the old theologians could find when they felt the need to go beyond what they could see to find some other source of truth. Like the whole of this journey, this now has to be understood in the light of what we have discovered about ourselves since. The idea that relationships are good for us makes sense to me. But this has so often been turned into an oppressive exclusivity.

The heterosexual and nuclear model of the family is no longer the only way that people find personal fulfilment. This is one of the great gifts of our modern society. To enable everyone to find a place as their humanity deserves, reasonable caring people, who never go near a church, now accept a greater variety in relationships than many people of faith seem happy with. Within that diverse human activity there are countless examples to be celebrated of love being given to and received from another person. 'God' is love. When we love we are expressing our fullest <u>human</u> nature; the depth of our being. That's what we should be talking about. Maybe that's as 'Sonlike' – as human – as we can ever become. Some of that love is between people of the same sex. Why not? How wonderful. Get over it!

But of course that's only half the story. Human relationships are also difficult to get right. Families can become closed and insular. Most abuse occurs there. Our modern world sometimes looks much more broken than in the past, but I suspect it is just that we are much more honest. I really do not believe the world was a better place at any time in the past than it is now. To my eyes we are far more compassionate as a species than is evidenced by the Old Testament or much of our later history. Have you ever actually read we used to do to our enemies, children, women? Remember Edward Wightman. Of course we have our own abominations but at least we see them as such. The moral temperature of a society does not seem very closely related to how much people identify with a religion. Indeed history suggests that religions have been just as much the cause of human unhappiness as offering a path towards its solution.

A God who 'became a man' only at one unique point in our history does not now seem to be the way that most helps us to do things better. At its best this theology sees God as suffering for us and with us; not the master at all but the servant. I get that. But much of that emphasis is lost in the doctrinal muddle of the Trinity. What really matters is the end product. Just my own 'salvation' transacted between God and Himself; or a human community in which the oppressed are set free, the sick healed, love is shared, and so on? This still rings true as an agenda that I don't want to turn my back on. That also seems to have been Jesus' primary concern, judging by the first sermon he gave. A God where a relationship within Himself is at the centre of things does not mean anything to me; but a focus on our relationships? – that's a different story and we need to go on telling it.

But it's just not necessary to create such an unholy Trinity in order to commit to making ourselves more whole, more inter-connected people. If I am still anywhere within the Christian community, perhaps I too am an Arian, or a Humanit-arian! Jesus the human is enough for me. There is no hope for a modern mind in relying on an external Deity to put things right between us or to sort it all out in some other life after this one. That's a key reason why the Christian story no longer grabs us. We have to do it ourselves, here and now. 'Love came down at Christmas' says the old carol. I beg to differ. Love was here all the time and still is. We just have to find it. (I'd say 'Love is all around' if others hadn't got there first!)

I still count myself in Jesus' family (just!) because, like him, I am human too. But I find it very hard to see him in the 'Christ' of the Church or as part of an eternal Godhead. That whole theology has removed him from the real world and placed us as the objects of a Divine subterfuge, hidden behind what actually happened, (see next Chapter). All we have to do is be grateful. But we don't need all these complex metaphysical ideas any more. We can seek, as best we can, to be more like what we know of Jesus, not simply sit back and admire the cosmic Christ or give up in despair. We can walk in his Way, share in his 'spirit of holiness', accept his challenge and turn the idea of personal fulfilment into reality. The Word can be 'made flesh', now, in us, not just in him. It's up to each of us to make him 'incarnate'. We do that by being the best son, daughter, parent, brother, sister, husband, wife, partner, carer, worker, citizen or friend that I would hope to be. To seek to become as fully human as Jesus was. We can embody his humanity as he embodied ours. This much I believe.

4   THE FOOL ON THE HILL

I believe ....'He suffered under Pontius Pilate, was
crucified, died and was buried....'

I first started to think about what eventually became this
Chapter a few days before Christmas 2012. At the time,
the news was dominated by one story; the shooting dead
of 20 children and 6 adults at a school in Connecticut by a
deranged young man with an assortment of high-powered
weapons that were owned by his mother, the first victim
of his spree. Inevitably it has faded from our minds, but
Christmas will never be the same again for those families
or for that small community. Not that such an event is
rare; it was the third school shooting that year in the USA,
and there have been plenty more since. As I have been
updating this, more mass killings have taken place, of
Jews, children and students. (Incidentally, the churches
are certainly fuller there than they are here and 40,000
people were shot dead last year). But this particular
massacre would have been mentioned in thousands of
genuine prayers for the victims and their families. Good
Christian people will have agonised at the pain of it all.

Some, given the timing, will have drawn a comparison
with the slaughter of the innocents that, according to

Matthew, followed the birth of Jesus. This would be understandable and has some point, even though King Herod's massacre almost certainly has no factual basis and is not evidenced in any other historical source as far as I am aware. It is just one of the many symbolic elements within the birth narratives, designed to show how Jesus of Nazareth was like a new Moses who would challenge the kingdoms of this world, not operate on an entirely different 'spiritual' plane away from the messy business of power and politics. Just as Pharaoh reacted to a perceived threat to his power by killing the baby Jewish boys, so did Herod.

Many believers will have asked, if not always when anyone else could hear, how their God could have 'allowed' such a thing to happen. Some will have blamed a devil. Neither response is a solution for me of course. A 'devil' is just another entirely human invention, (and not mentioned in the story of the Garden of Eden, though I have heard it said many times). Human beings are entirely responsible for such behaviour, whether it's the lack of gun control, the result of fragmented relationships or whatever causes people to sometimes lose all sense of reason and become mad. There is no God or devil who we can hold to account for such insanity. It's just part of the package, like love, sunshine and Chopin.

If I had been preaching that weekend, as I used to do every Sunday, I would have spoken especially about the teachers. Schools rather than churches have been my world in recent years. I can still recall the day in 1996 when Thomas Hamilton walked into the primary school in Dunblane and killed 16 children and their teacher. I vividly remember how the children in the Sunday School I was connected with then lined up in tears to sign their names in a book of condolence. I had never been more proud of them. There was a similar, if less destructive event in the city where I now live around the same time. There too the bravery of a young woman teacher saved more children from being injured and almost certain death. Terrible things happen every day, every hour, every minute. Like everyone else, I can only make myself aware of some of them.

Without doubt, at least one of the teachers in the Connecticut shooting deliberately surrendered her own life in order to save some of her pupils. She locked them in a storeroom and went back towards the danger to try and save some more. She then put herself between the gunman and a group of 6 year-olds who were cowering in a corner and died protecting them.I am staggered by such an action and not at all sure I could ever hope to do anything like the same myself. I have no idea whether she was a Christian, quite possibly she was. But of course it doesn't matter one bit. There is no greater love. 'Inasmuch as you do it for the least of these my brothers and sisters, you do it for me', irrespective of the person's religious faith or motivation. All other considerations are irrelevant.

Alongside this wholly inadequate tribute, I would have talked about Jesus. Not, as in the sermon I actually heard that week, using the USA massacre just to prove what a cruel and wicked world this is and that you had better put your trust in him as your only hope, rather than wallowing in the sentimentality of the stable. (That'll encourage them to come back again next year!) For me, the death of Jesus is a paradigm of <u>self-sacrifice</u>: a demonstration of love for others that joins this particular Christmas to Good Friday and makes the actions of those teachers a genuinely 'sacramental' moment. I saw exactly the same truth in the picture of the three women caring for the soldier killed outside Woolwich barracks, just as other women did for Jesus at the cross. We saw it again in the humanitarian response by local people in offering help to those who couldn't get home after the Manchester Arena bomb or following the fire at Grenfell tower. These signs of human compassion in the face of such cruelty or disaster give me more hope than a million evangelical sermons demanding that I be 'saved' ever will.

Many might consider such self-denying behaviour foolish and pointless but it is surely evidence of a much greater wisdom about the way things are? Part of the lingering attraction of Christianity, perhaps rather bizarrely, is the kind of death that is at the heart of it and the response that it still evokes, even in me. It's the usual supernatural meaning that is placed upon it that I cannot affirm. This was not a staged or prearranged sacrifice between a God and Himself. It was a barbaric act of human wickedness – within which we have to find some hope or meaning if it is to be anything more than that. The key point about the figure at the centre of this human death is that he was indeed a victim of <u>our</u> inhumanity. People like us killed him, not God. The cross is an emblem of death, and of the particularly savage way of doing it by crucifixion, not a 'religious' symbol at all.

This event 'earths' all spirituality in the reality of the human condition in a way that still makes a connection to me, at least on one level. The cross is such an enduring image in early Christianity that there can be little doubt that this really was how Jesus of Nazareth died. There is a famous graffito in the catecombs in Rome that shows a man kneeling before a cross with a donkey's head on it: 'Alexamenos worships his god'. There would have been no reason to invent such an embarrassment and it could have been easily disproved if it did not happen and Jesus actually died in his sleep as an old man. Most religions go for myths that build up their central figures; they don't portray them as a condemned and broken man dying on a rubbish dump.

Jesus' death fits with what else I know to be true about life: good people die, often unjustly. That's a fact. This event makes other deaths of the same kind more significant and worth something. They reinforce the value of his and he illuminates theirs. This all gives the deaths a meaning as they deserve and shows that those who fail to be fully human don't have things all their own way. But I simply cannot accept what was done with this death afterwards, by Paul and especially by Augustine and Luther, rather than by those who were there at the time. I don't believe the real Jesus has anything more to do with the subsequent Christ of the Church than he does with the eternal second person of the Trinity that I failed to find in Chapter 3. This later Christ-figure is solely the creation of a community who were up against it and needed a reassurance of their own survival.

The Roman historian Tacitus wrote about how the bodies of Christians on crosses were set alight to provide flaming torches in Rome during the reign of

Nero. They were said to be responsible for the fires that almost destroyed the city so he devised a suitably cruel punishment in response. This is the reality of crucifixion that came to dominate their memory of Jesus and turned the message about him into something wholly original. Jesus was, for them, the longed-for Jewish Messiah, even if not in the way that was anticipated. But as they too faced the reality of persecution, the need for a Saviour who would rescue and reward the faithful, even beyond death, took over from the memory of the fool on the hill who chose to be crucified rather than compromise his vision for a new kind of religion. That was an inspiration to those who came after him, and to me, but they added a dimension of meaning that I just don't believe was there.

Building on a reinterpretation of Old Testament texts, a whole new understanding of the death of Jesus was constructed which was certainly not what the original prophecies meant. They all looked forward to a new nation; a new human community, as Jews still do. But that was no longer the focus. This is where all the emphasis on Jesus being a sacrifice comes from – yet again a direct result of the human experiences that came with being his follower, not the driver that created them. The cross does not feature in the original Messianic promises. But New Testament Christianity took the old scriptures and transformed them into something else.

The context was entirely different once the story left its Jewish roots and hit the Greek-speaking world where the original Messianic expectation did not exist. Now we had a new Jesus; a Christ. It's the same word as 'Messiah' (translated into Greek) but it doesn't have the same

Jewish meaning as before. Individual 'salvation' now became the focus, not a hope for the nation's liberation and renewal. Now Jesus' death was all about God doing something, not the Romans. But is there any basis for such a conviction? Only by creating something out of this death that wasn't there at the time.

Jesus of Nazareth died because he chose not to keep quiet about the way the religion of his day had turned into an oppressive and exclusive club that had totally distorted what he believed his God wanted for the world. He was a convenient scapegoat and it suited all those in power to offer him up, as so many have done with others since. (The massive irony is that the Church that bears his name has so often done exactly the same over the subsequent years). As the Creeds actually make explicit, but then totally ignore, this all happened because of the human players in the drama. Jesus died, not because of any supernatural pulling of strings, but because he upset the religious establishment of his time who persuaded a weak Roman governor to have him killed to keep the peace. This is the true historical and factual reason for his death. It happens all the time. There are Pontius Pilates all over our modern world. Any response has to begin there. Perhaps it should end there too.

I have to accept that I wouldn't even know about this death had it not been for the later Christ of the Church. Without that continuing story, his execution would be just one more name in the catalogue of human misery; just another death. But perhaps challenging that anonymity is part of the point. Millions die without being noticed. A while ago I was in Cambodia and heard all about the torture and killing of thousands under Pol Pot. During the late 1970s, the entire city of Phnom Penh was emptied and all the intellectuals, lawyers, artists, journalists and teachers executed. We visited the former school, turned into a prison, in which the atrocities took place on an unimaginable scale. Their blood was still on the floor. There were hundreds of photographs of the victims. Like the Romans, the Khmer Rouge were very efficient and bureaucratic killers; they photographed everyone before they executed them. But the relatives of those who died have maintained their memory. As our guide explained, whose own father was killed there, they have refuted their anonymity by keeping their family members' pictures on display for all to see. I found that immensely moving.

The New Testament chronicles how the followers of Jesus, or more accurately, new followers who hadn't been there before, kept his memory alive. That's actually why even I still sometimes receive the Eucharist; to do the same. But they also went on to create an understanding of his death that took the experience on to a whole new level. I suppose I should be grateful to them. But were they justified in doing so? That is a monumentally significant question. Did they make an entirely different 'Jesus' out of this particular death, or did they come to see what was really going on behind the scenes?

I do not believe that God sent Jesus to his death so that we can be 'saved'. There are so many levels at which this idea is frankly immoral as well as unbelievable and, more importantly, I really do not see how such an understanding of his death helps us. The killings go on. The world has not become a better place as a result of this

Divine act, let alone the sheer intellectual impossibility of believing in a God who has to separate Himself into both priest and victim on this particular sacrificial altar. Such imagery might have made sense in the Middle East 2000 years ago. It means nothing to me in C21st Britain.

Christians also usually affirm that the only hope in this situation lies in its uniqueness. This was a 'once for all' event that changed the relationship between us and God forever, (assuming, of course, that we believe that such a gulf actually exists in the first place). The death of Jesus is entirely different from all other deaths, because Jesus is different from all other human beings – he is also God. In contrast, I would say that the only hope is in the fact that he is the <u>same</u>. That Jesus and me and the victims of the holocaust and Pol Pot, the Connecticut teachers, the random targets of ISIS <u>and</u> those who do the killing, all share a common humanity. Otherwise anything he did does not relate to a mere mortal like me. The hope comes in the light that such an event spreads into my own experience, not that it is uniquely different from it.

Despite the tragedy of such deaths, the world is not a universally awful place. Quite the reverse is true according to what Jesus had to say about the reality of his God to be found within it. The executions are balanced by the love and self-sacrifices; the selfishness by the generosity; the oppression by the willingness of some to put others first rather than themselves. But such deaths should never be minimised. The human Jesus shared in this too. He did not sail serenely through Gethsemane knowing that God was holding all the cards on his behalf and all would be well in the end. My guess is that he was as petrified as anyone else would be when confronted by a murderous mob. If he was somehow above it all, what would his death have to offer us, assuming, as I do, that this is not about a God at all, but just about ourselves and how we treat one another?

We are fortunate that from our modern perspective we can discern at least something of the factual basis behind the later elaborations. This was nothing like so available before the insights of historical research into the Biblical text. It's a pity that so many religious people today take no notice of it. They effectively miss out the first three gospels, which focus on Jesus' teaching, and jump straight to John and Paul, passing over much of what the real Jesus stood for along the way. There is little or no evidence within the synoptic gospels that suggests Jesus' underlying intention, and that which made it all worthwhile, was to save me from my sins. Jesus' focus was on the 'kingdom'; the rule of his God on earth here and now. His teaching was about that, not about himself, (see next Chapter).

There are certainly signs that he came to see his death as of some greater significance. Given the Messianic expectations that were around at the time, it seems likely that he believed that by following his path to the end he would usher in some new age – a fulfilment of the Old Testament prophecies which clearly meant so much to him. We must never forget that, whatever we have done with him since, he was a Jew. Jesus was not a Christian! We get far closer to understanding him by reading Isaiah than we do by reading Paul or the early Church Fathers. It may just be possible to believe that there was something else going on as well as, but not instead of the historical reality. The question is, which one now speaks to us with any meaning? Jesus as the victim of human cruelty who stands alongside us as one of us, or Jesus the tool of a God who just used Him(self), and those around him, for some greater purpose? The edifice of later religious interpretation only obscures the actual meaning as far as I am concerned.

So what happened after the cross? And what will happen to me? I cannot, of course, believe that a personal resurrection can be some kind of hope for the future out of all this disaster, not for Jesus or for me, or not at least in any literal sense. To go back again to what actually happened, I strongly suspect there was no tomb. The story about Joseph of Arimathea having one available is just too convenient. Jesus' body was probably just left to rot or thrown into a communal pit like all the others. The 'resurrection of the body' is absent both from my pilgrimage through the Apostles' Creed and my journey through life. Death is the end – how can I possibly believe anything else this side of it? Any kind of 'afterlife' is just another human theory. The New Testament writers' attempts to describe the indescribable again fall back on stories that, like the birth narratives, don't really work as fact. Did the resurrected Jesus still have a physical body that could only be in one place at once? The allegedly empty tomb and the encounter with Thomas suggest so. If so, what happened to it? 'Heaven' is not 'up'. But the stories are inconsistent.

The risen Jesus also seems not to have been immediately recognisable as the same person as before. Some of those he met didn't realise who he was. He 'appeared' in locked rooms or suddenly disappeared from view. Luke's 'appearances' are all in and around Jerusalem; in Matthew the disciples are back in Galilee. These images cannot all be reconciled. But that's OK because that's all they are; just human creations to try and express something much deeper. Is it essential to believe in any kind of bodily resurrection in order to see his death as having value for us? I don't think so. The hope has to be found <u>within</u> the death, not by somehow passing over to it to something better. The good news the disciples first affirmed was in seeing the present in a new way, not in a longing for some future reward somewhere else. That all came later.

My life will be over when I am dead and I do not believe that it was any different for Jesus, the real human man from Nazareth. Surely the words that were remembered as spoken on the cross tell us that he too saw his dying as an ending? 'Into your hands I commend my spirit.' 'It is finished'. This is certainly a fulfilment, a completion; but not a transition to some other kind of existence. That has to be entirely speculative. This is not to deny that Jesus' first disciples, and his followers today, had some genuine experience of his continuing presence, but it is a human feeling; an activity of our brains like any other, like love for someone, which can still be there even after they have died. When the disciples began to discover that his death was not the end of their story after all, it was <u>as if</u> Jesus was alive in them, (rather similar to a Confucian idea of reality devised just a few hundred years earlier).

Others who had never known Jesus then came to believe the same, but those who had actually known him disappear from the story almost immediately. The Christ of the Church is a different kind of 'reality' but as before, it can only be a continuing metaphorical presence that they affirmed, based on their human experience. A meaning that requires empty tombs, ascending bodies and seats in heaven cannot be a believable truth in a world of scientific rationality, for Jesus or for anyone else. Dead men do not walk and to make Jesus the only ever exception in history really does not help us. But there are other kinds of meanings to be found. My father lives on in my life today; I have been enormously influenced by many people who are no longer alive. Some people change the world. Hope does indeed spring eternal. Magnificent victories can come from what looks like total defeat. Joy comes in the morning, at least sometimes. All of this is a kind of resurrection, if not what Christians usually mean by the word.

If I am asked 'Does the death of Jesus make any difference'?, I think I can say 'yes'. It makes a difference to my understanding of tragedies like the Connecticut shootings and the crimes of Pol Pot. I still find Good Friday an immensely meaningful day, but Remembrance Day and Holocaust Memorial Day can be almost as significant. Words like 'Surely he has borne our griefs and carried our sorrows?' still touch me at a deeper level than most things do. They are indeed ours; a part of us from which there is no escape. Others have called that 'sin'. To me it is just part of the human deal that sits alongside the best. Take either away and we would no longer be human. The killing of Jesus – it's interesting that we don't normally use that phrase, it wasn't just a death – brings home a reality about the human condition that must not be ignored. There is a truth here, even if it is not about somehow changing my eternal status with a God I do not believe is there.

So I still want to be the foot of the cross in some sense, acknowledging the significance of this particular death, if only as a representative of all the others. Many people, much greater than me, have also given their lives in equally cruel circumstances. There is no deliverance from such things, not here and not for those left behind when all of this is over for each of us, but they can be put in their place. By still telling the Jesus story, if without all the doctrinal trimmings that came later, I am recognising the importance and value of _life_ and acknowledging that suffering, especially of the unjust sort, is simply inescapable.

In what happened to Jesus I can see that sadness and death are an integral part of what it means to be alive, but they are not all there is to say. The cross is an enduring symbol of all that and I still want to identify with it as a vindication that all such acts of cruelty are not entirely devoid of hope. The death of Jesus helps me to make some sense out of my own life and to keep going in the face of all this world's gross injustices. Perhaps this all still seems foolish. But his death still matters and I want to go on recognising the reality of it. This much I believe.

5   A MATTER OF JUDGEMENT

I believe....'He will come again to judge the living and the dead...'.

If you were able to tell Peter or Paul that there were still Christians in an obscure north-western corner of the former Roman Empire 20 centuries later, they would certainly be immensely surprised and probably not a little disappointed. They would not have anticipated that we would all still be here. The first Christians very quickly turned their eyes to the immediate future, rather than only retelling the stories of the past. Jesus had spoken in apocalyptic terms about the coming of the kingdom; that there were those listening to him who would actually see it. So they believed that something dramatic would happen imminently to change the way things were; within no more than a few years, possibly even within their own lifetimes.

What was expected to happen next became the dominant theme of the New Testament, especially in the early writings of Paul, parts of the synoptic Gospels (that came after, not before Paul) and the later writings of the Johns who wrote the fourth Gospel and the book of Revelation. Jesus would be coming back. The imagery quickly became concerned with the end of things as we know them, not with a world that has carried on pretty much the same ever since. Given the persecution that the Christians received almost from the very beginning, initially from the Jews but primarily from the Romans, this emphasis on a future hope of something radically different is hardly surprising. Again, it entirely fits its social context as religions always will. The belief grew out of the experience. The faithful were dying; surely that couldn't be right? Hadn't Jesus promised that they would be redeemed? How could this be if they were already dead and buried? There must be some final event pending that would put it all right and make sure that the bad guys got what was coming to them. God's sense of justice demands it.

But as the cross and all those other deaths like it surely show, it's not as simple as that. Things are altogether more muddled. Bad things happen to good people, and vice versa. I would argue that we can find a real sense of liberation once we accept that's just how things are. We don't need to create a God to tidy things up. But for those who do believe it, a strong sense of mutual reassurance that we have backed the right horse may be all that keeps the demons of despair away when the going gets tough. Then as now there were those who formed themselves into semi-secret societies or underground movements and waited for the coming 'rapture'. Others took up arms against the occupying forces to try and hasten the end times or gave up sex and distributed all their property to others because they believed they would no longer need it where they were going. Such groups were common in the

1st century world and the early Jewish Christians quickly found a home within such an environment.

The problem is, it didn't happen. And it never will. I am as confident of that as I am about anything. This was not, in the view of many scholars, ever the kind of crisis that Jesus meant. Even by the time of the Creeds this had become a distant expectation, except as reinterpreted to focus on the eventual destiny of each individual. Centuries had passed without Jesus' return and the early convictions had to be revised in the light of it. Many more have passed since and, hopefully, there will be many more to come. There may well be an end to things one day; everything else in the Universe is finite as far as we know. But there is absolutely no meaningful basis to any claim that it will be 'soon'. It has, after all, been 'soon' for 2000 years according to those who still turn to the New Testament for simplistic predictions of what is about to happen. History is full of groups who sat and waited.....only for nothing to occur. Some see the current conflict in the Middle East as a sign of a coming Armageddon, but they are surely wrong. There are a few who are actively hoping for it; they are positively dangerous.

Terrifying, world-shattering, cataclysmic events have occurred right throughout history; tens of millions have died in massacres, famines, epidemics and natural disasters. Atom bombs have been exploded and global wars fought. Tyrannies have risen and fallen again. The world has been littered with crucifixions. And we are still going strong, even if we also shows signs of abusing our planet to excess. Only a massive change in the Universe along the lines of the one that brought it all into being will end it all again, and even that might only be in our small corner. Maybe it will happen sometime. Maybe there will be new ice ages or dramatically rising sea levels. But that will be nothing to do with a God. There is no logic in believing it's about to happen now, given the thousands of millions of years that have gone before us. It is one of the most irrational elements of faith to suggest otherwise, though I can see how some people might be still be attracted to it, if they think it will be for their own personal benefit.

Maintaining the fiction of an imminent final judgement used to be almost the sole preoccupation of organised Christianity. At first it was that graves will be opened, Jesus will 'descend' (from where?) and you'd best be ready. Then people were told that they had better believe before it was too late for them personally. Graphic illustrations of eternal torment took pride of place in ancient cathedrals. If you want to make yourself feel really ill, read some of the hellfire sermons of Jonathan Edwards, (the C18[th] one, not the former triple-jumper who refused to compete on a Sunday and who, incidentally, is now an atheist). Endless liturgies were created that were designed to keep God happy, to intercede for the faithful and to make sure that His coming wrath was directed elsewhere. Even believing at the very last minute would do, or you could buy the expensive 'indulgences' that would protect either you or your relatives in the afterlife. Or you had better accept every word of Scripture and invite Jesus to be your own Personal Lord and Saviour and be 'born again'; just turning up at church and living a good life isn't enough. Etcetera. Etcetera.

Of course it might still be claimed that it will all happen to me when I die, but given that my body will be burnt to ashes and scattered into the sea or returned to the earth in a woodland somewhere, I really do not see how. There will be nothing left of me to be punished or rewarded. An eternal 'soul' is just another human theory. I am intrigued that some people even now refuse to be cremated on the grounds that they will need their bodies for some future resurrection. Have they ever seriously thought about the impossibility of such an idea? Of all the claims of all the religions this is the most deceitful and thankfully most people, even many of those who believe at least some of the rest, have let it go. This understanding of a Judgement Day should be left where it belongs – in our more superstitious past along with burning lakes of brimstone, goblins and little red devils with very sharp tridents. However, what we must <u>not</u> let go of is the need to make decisions about how to live or begin to think that it no longer matters. There is a judgement to be made, but this side of death not beyond it. These decisions, and the responsibility for making them, belong to us, not to some external Deity.

Many people of faith assume that we can only know anything about human values because they come to us from a God. The most common response I have to my own position is 'If there is no God then there is no right or wrong laid down and anything goes'. I have never understood this. Why do the most important things about us have to come from somewhere else? Does my ability to enjoy music, or my appreciation of beautiful scenery and the warmth of the sunshine have to come from a God? Can they not just be part of me; part of being alive? Similarly, when deciding about how life is to be lived, it's actually <u>our</u> sense of justice that is in play here. The notion of a God who will ride over the horizon like the cavalry coming to the rescue of the beleaguered wagon-train was an entirely understandable response to powerlessness, but it reflects our own natural desire to see right prevail, not some expectation that has to come from Someone else if it's ever going to happen. Like everything else, it's down to us. These are our desires projected onto the gods, not the other way round.

We have created these so-called 'God-given' standards in the first place. Where else can they have come from? This is the point to which I keep returning; Virgil's question. Everything we claim to be true about a God; every scripture and religious book that has ever been written, every commandment ever observed or 'spiritual' experience ever felt; every temple and church ever built and every creed and moral code ever taught, has been created by us. So we can change our understanding of them. Indeed we have to do so in the light of our evolving human knowledge, just as we no longer teach our children that the sun goes round the earth or that there are fairies at the bottom of the garden. What is it about religious ideas that makes them exempt from this process of greater enlightenment? Science has moved us on but God has apparently stood still.

When it comes to medicine, for example, we embrace the new with enthusiasm. We no longer need to be the powerless victims of illnesses and diseases. We can take them on and even beat them thanks to the insights of recent discoveries. I would be dead already if we hadn't developed such knowledge. But when it comes to religion and morality we are often told that we are stuck forever in the understandings of a different age, subject to a judgement based on the standards laid down centuries ago in an entirely different context. A supernatural God and His ways are not the source of our wish to build a better world or our desire to see good prosper; they are a reflection of that desire within ourselves. These human 'gods' need not be selfish ones as most conventional believers seem to assume. Why have people written such ideals into virtually every religion there is? Because we believe in them! We have traditionally put these sentiments onto a God in order to validate them, (though ironically the consequences have often been dreadful injustices perpetrated in His name), but we no longer need to do so for them to be 'true'.

We got there first, before the religions we then created to reinforce what we wanted to see happen. This is so important to the debate about believing. Justice, truth, love and so on are not Divine characteristics that we can't possibly hope to live by. They're not values that have to be imposed upon us. They weren't written on tablets of stone handed down from the sky. They're <u>our</u> characteristics in the first place and the religions we have devised are designed (by and large) to promote them because we know that they are good for us. Certainly, as the previous Chapter made clear, we are also competitive animals who have the potential to be as brutal as the rest of nature can be. But we also know that the way of everlasting conflict doesn't actually make us happy. It is in everyone's best interests for the human community to get along together and to challenge the things that divide us. Why can't this just be part of a 'natural' law rather than a supernatural one?

Personally I see the truth of this, in part at least, because of what Jesus of Nazareth seemed to say about the 'kingdom', along, of course, with others who have spoken of similar ideals and lived them out where they happen to be. No one religious or philosophical tradition can claim an exclusive insight here, but Christianity is the one I know most about so that's where my thinking is still directed. Nearly everyone agrees that the 'kingdom' was the dominant theme of Jesus' message before the Church turned him into something else. There are signs that he came to believe that its 'coming' was somehow bound up with his own death. But it is only later interpretations that reframe his message entirely in terms of a personal salvation dependant on a particular faith in him or on some unspecified 'second' coming and Final Judgement when all will be revealed.

It was for him a kingdom (or, better, an 'on-going rule') of his God, but that language of Divinity does not mean that what he had to say is irrelevant to me. The images and metaphors change; the insights behind them may be more enduring. We used to explain many things by reference to a God that we now explain in other ways. But it still rains just the same, however we understand its cause. Religion is a way to explain what goes on anyway, not a different kind of experience that is only accessible to those who have some secret insight that the rest of us haven't found. You say tomato. I say a reddish fruit that grows in greenhouses and tastes great on a pizza. Same difference when it comes to eating it.

But Jesus' vision of a God, and of the world, were like no other before. Most of the time he specifically avoids talking about what we might now call 'religion'; neither does he look to Churches, priests or creeds for his inspiration and examples. He talks about <u>life</u>; human life, real life – people, jobs, relationships, farming and so on. He invited (not told) his hearers to open their eyes and look again at what was going on around them and see it all in a new way. The rule of his God was to be found there. There is an inescapable challenge to be faced here. But the results of this judgement are not what most people would have expected. This is a Jesus who belongs as much, if not more, to people like me than to those who claim to be his spokesmen – to outsiders, sinners, doubters and those of very little significance to the holy powers that be. Religious people beware. Be careful what you wish for!

A good place to look for more about all this is the whole series of parables that appear in Matthew's gospel, Chapters 24-25. It's well worth getting a Bible out if you have one and reading them through – Matthew is the first book of the New Testament (in the traditional order), though not the first to be written. Matthew's gospel, like the others, has to be approached with some caution as it clearly reflects the needs of the community for which it was written, rather than necessarily preserving exactly what Jesus said and meant a generation or more earlier. Their own current situation as outsiders within Judaism is almost certainly the context to which the writer is referring, not only that of Jesus. But we have to work with what we have and this is as close as I can get.

The stories are about the coming of the 'Son of Man', (e.g. Chapter 24 v.37). No-one quite knows what this title means. It is only later thinking that assumes that Jesus was referring to himself. Matthew almost certainly thought so. But the term comes from the book of Daniel, a late Old Testament book that was already contributing to the generally apocalyptic climate at the time. Originally it was certainly not about Jesus, but he may have identified with the figure, looking back. His use of it may have had something to do with the vindication of past Jewish martyrs or he may have adopted the term as a kind of code by which he could criticise the occupying Romans without them realising its significance. There is little doubt that he was heightening a sense of immediate crisis. The whole dramatic point is that no-one can tell when great decisive events will happen. The kingdom moment is now. These teachings are about a feature of present reality; not merely a future hope.

The basis of this existential moment of judgement is also entirely unexpected. No-one can predict the timing, or the outcome. Each day is a day of judgement. It is ever-present. We could say that every day is a 'second coming' if you want to hold on to such a belief. Doesn't the Christian believe that Jesus is constantly inviting them to walk with him, not standing in the distance beckoning while they catch up? Surely your God's rule is already here? And his conclusions, right throughout his parables, turn most usual religious convictions on their heads. The sinners see this reality in advance of the righteous people. People are not in the Temple when the moment comes; they're in the fields or on their housetops. Those who are welcomed to the King's side are those who were so busy doing good that they didn't even realise the significance of what they were doing. Their motivation had absolutely nothing to do with God as far as they were aware – they just did it.

To Jesus' original hearers these were all (not very) veiled attacks on the priests and the interpreters of the law who had turned the whole religious enterprise into a kind of 'self-preservation society'. When it was supposed to be all about being a 'light to the Gentiles'; about breaking down barriers not creating them; about setting people free, not tying them up in doctrinal knots and only letting them go if they could recite all the right passwords first. That way is not evidence of the rule of God, as Jesus understood it. That is the more selfish side of ourselves against which we need to be constantly struggling. And it was ruthlessly exploited as the Church later became ever more powerful. But the actual judgement involved is all about whether we have discovered the 'signs' of the kingdom and lived in ways that draw out our true potential and enable us to make the world a better place, not just to stand in condemnation over it. That's what's at stake, and the religious leaders of Jesus' time, he said, were rubbish at it! Maybe not much has changed since.

Those who are big on judgement days, especially the Big One waiting around the corner, seem to me to have entirely missed the point. It is a depressing fact that the more 'religious' you are and the more you talk about Jesus as your 'Saviour', the more it seems to lead you into a conservative morality and an attitude of criticism towards those who are different from yourself. This is entirely against the concept of discovering the hidden kingdom around us. It is the very opposite of what Jesus talked about. Indeed it is the failing for which he was so hard on those of his own time who claimed to know it all. Why is so much that many Church leaders say always so negative? It's like the story of the bishop visiting a church and an old man telling him he's been coming there for over 60 years. 'You must have seen some changes in that time', says the bishop. 'Yes' replies the old man, 'and I've been against every one of them!' Their judgement is so often hostile. The world is going to hell in a hand-cart. 'Secularism' is destroying us. Moral standards are declining. Change is always for the worse. Nothing better ever comes from what was there before. 'We're all doomed'!

The Archbishop of Canterbury once argued that non-religious schools lack any moral compass and are, by definition, less value-based than Church schools. (He had to apologise later). That must be why adults keep coming forward to disclose the abuse they suffered at the hands of priests, clergy, nuns etc. or in strict Jewish schools and madrasas. It is a massive insult to those whose morality is based on a collective humanism rather than any Theism. It's the same with so many other moral changes and new thinking. The knee-jerk Christian reaction is so often to be against it, because it comes from the 'world' not from their God or their scriptures. But maybe the 'world' is where the real hope is coming from. The 'kingdom' is to be found there, at least according to Jesus. There might actually be some sources of truth to be found among us there that will get us closer to where we need to be, or rather, give us a clearer understanding of where we already are.

This is another reason why religion can so often seem to be irrelevant. All it ever seems to say to us is how hopeless we are without it. Well, I hate to disagree but there are ample signs that we still have all kinds of values as part of our humanity which may be even more like the ones religions are supposed to be about, not less. 'Judgement' is not about getting ready for a future cosmic event in which Jesus will leap from the clouds and come up to people like me and say' I told you so'. Neither is it about scaring me into a social or moral conformity that suits some powerful elite on pain of dire consequences when I am dead. I am absolutely convinced that neither of these ideas was uppermost in the mind of Jesus.

Of course this is my own interpretation and many wouldn't share it. As I have already discussed, if you take the whole New Testament into account the emphasis about Jesus clearly changes. I can't call myself a 'Christian' because I respond to him in this way. (I actually have no wish to do so). But I am struck by the emphasis that appears to me to be there at the start and which is very different from what I hear or see in many of the churches that bear his name. As I will try to explore a bit further in the next Chapter, it seems you can't have a religion without a church. But I wonder if we can live life to the full and face each moment of judgement as it comes, but without any religion to help us? Alain de Botton has explored such an idea in several of his books.

I acknowledge a need to be constantly evaluating my life and what really counts within it. I have to make decisions and choices on a daily basis and need to do so with integrity. A healthy self-judgement is continually required as a benchmark, and it helps to do it with others. There is absolutely no room for complacency and not just anything goes. That would be immature naivety and self-indulgent sentimentality, unsupported by an often messy reality. But my shared humanity is there to feed my search for what is right, not inevitably to lead me astray. Many 'religious' values have in fact lost sight of what we are capable of becoming. I genuinely think we can often do better without them. It's the 'kingdom' values that count. You can't just look them up in a book of rules or ask someone else to decide for you, though I hope Part 2 will help. Of course, working out what it all means will always be a matter of judgement. But this much I believe.

6   CALLED TO BE SAINTS

'I believe in the holy catholic church.. (and) the communion of saints.'

I have borrowed this Chapter's title from one of my mother's books, (who herself borrowed it from the New Testament). At this point the Apostles' Creed moves onto my territory or at least a bit closer to it. This is not a statement of faith in a God, or His Son and what he supposedly did by dying, or about what is claimed to be true about the past, present or the future. Those who recite the Creed are asked not to look heavenward at this point but to look at each other. In contrast to all the rest, it is saying that we believe in ourselves; it's about believing in human communities of which churches are supposed to be exemplars. At last, something positive about our humanity.

And it doesn't say 'I believe in kings, politicians or the editors of newspapers'; not even bishops or Popes! Looking at our own context, and in line with all those saints who have gone before us, 'Church' is one thing about us that we can put our faith in. Well, maybe! The 'catholic' Church being referred to here is not, of course, just the 'Roman Catholic' denomination, though that was the only Western church at the time the Creed was written and the word may still cause some confusion. All Christians in this country were RCs once, until Henry VIII decided to set up his own alternative Church and make himself the head of it so that he could grant himself a divorce. (What a delicious irony given the attitude of some clergy to those whose marriages fail today).

The Church's own history, just like its beliefs and scriptures, reflects an entirely human enterprise, perhaps more clearly here than anywhere else. It's important to remember that your historic medieval cathedral or Norman C of E building in the village centre would have been an RC church until 500 years ago. The Creeds are, in that sense, 'Roman' Creeds, though that might not be very comfortable for some of those who still affirm belief in them. I have been into church buildings where the whole inside was once facing in the opposite direction; alterations that reflected the fashions and politics of the time, as well as strictly religious preferences. Churches are mirrors of our human journey, and not just our 'spiritual' one. Change has always been a part of it. Sometimes that's involved a complete about-turn – hold that thought!

'Catholic' in this sense has the same meaning as when we describe someone as having 'catholic' tastes. They enjoy lots of different things. The Church must have variety within it. It is not a statement about uniformity and authority; about everyone having to be subject to the control of hierarchies and leaders, but the complete opposite. Churches should demonstrate 'catholicity', which I understand as meaning that there should be room for everyone. A diversity within the unity. That's what believers are saying they believe in.

As the Creed reminds us, there is also a solidarity with those who have gone before and the Church's early history is especially instructive here. 'Christianity' began as a small Jewish sect, not as an entirely separate religion. The writer of the Acts of the Apostles tells us that they carried on worshipping in the Jewish way, but also met to remember Jesus by breaking bread together as he had instructed. They shared things in common and supported those who had been widowed, possibly by martyrdom. Or maybe the community particularly attracted women, several of whom also seem to have been key members of the Jesus community before and after his death, judging by their prominent roles in the resurrection stories, (often overlooked). Some would say that this was the Church's finest hour, a kind of new Garden of Eden, but it didn't last for long.

Judaism was already a pretty diverse community. The Pharisees and the Sadducees were hardly on speaking terms, but at least they retained a sense of being part of the same tradition. Then there were the groups we know as 'Essenes'; more separatist and radical in their rejection of both the Roman occupation and the official worship in the Temple and who tended to do their own thing in remote locations. The Dead Sea scrolls are almost certainly an insight into their semi-monastic way of life, based in a community at Qumran near the western shores of the Dead Sea. Then there were the Zealots who wanted to throw the Romans out by violence. The synagogues and the Jerusalem Temple had to find room for them all.

The new Jesus sect fitted pretty well into this version of catholicity for a while. His disciples may even have been consciously chosen to reflect this variety. They were known as followers of 'The Way', or the 'Nazarenes' according to Luke's account of the run up to Paul's conversion. Perhaps 'ordinary' Jews in particular were attracted to them, as a contrast to the rather stiff formalism that Jesus himself had also apparently found so unsatisfactory. His followers were, after all, mostly those from outside the conventional religious establishment. Some of them may well have been those who had been previously attracted to John the Baptist. What happened to all those he had baptised? Some experts argue that this was the path chosen by James, Jesus' brother, who later became the leader of the community in Jerusalem even though he wasn't apparently one of Jesus' former closest disciples.

Within a few years, Jesus groups sprang up further north – though we don't know how exactly they got there or who was responsible for this expansion – to Galilee, Damascus and, crucially Antioch, then the capital of Syria and the third most important city of the Roman empire according to scholars. This is where they were first given the nickname of 'Christians'. This was also when the sect started to engage with non-Jews; Gentiles. For some it seems that this pushed the tolerance of diversity too far. Gentiles were different; not any part of God's 'chosen' people. The Pharisee Saul was despatched to sort them out having already taken at least the role of spectator in the stoning of Stephen for going beyond what was acceptable. As we know, Saul saw the error of his ways on the way there. He became Paul; the gamekeeper turned poacher and the rest, as they say, is history.

But over the next few years as the Gentile world started to embrace the new message about Jesus, there was still a massive debate going on within the young churches about how far things should go. Acts suggests that the Jerusalem church and Paul frequently fell out and they had to work hard at finding some kind of reconciliation. They organised at least one summit to agree how to work together. The results weren't entirely conclusive but Paul more or less won the day, somewhat helped by the destruction of the Jerusalem Temple in 70CE, and his wider vision was accepted. But his letters to the churches around the Mediterranean are often about the arguments that continued among and between them.

Did you have to be a Jew first in order to become a Christian? Were the Jewish Christians somehow better than the rest? What about circumcision, the food laws or still engaging in other religious cults at the same time? Did Gentile Christians have to accept all the Jewish scriptures and live by all the requirements of the Mosaic Law? And what about those interested enquirers who just wanted to be semi-observers but without actually committing themselves? Did that really count as belonging? Like the much later debates about the Trinity, these were not just polite discussions between academics. Paul can be strident in his criticisms and although we have only his half of the correspondence, it is clear that they didn't always take much notice of his advice and had to be told again! By the time of the book of Revelation, the writer is even more critical of the churches' failings.

Once we get to the Creeds, people were being condemned for heresy or excommunicated all over the place. Most of the 4th century was taken up with the Arian controversy about Jesus' relationship with God. Bishops were removed from office and exiled. Strong letters were sent and more argumentative meetings held, all over whether or not the Son was of 'one substance' with the Father. The idea that the Son was part of the created order was supposedly rejected by the Council of Nicea in 325, but the dispute ranged on for decades. It was clearly a very mixed picture. 'How these Christians love one another', wrote Tertullian. It is thought that no irony was intended despite all these disagreements; they genuinely did also provide a model of mutual love and support, not least in the face of unjust persecution and deprivations. But when you look at Northern Ireland, or the way some traditionalists have behaved towards radical theologians or those of a different sexuality, modern observers can't help at least a wry smile at such a statement.

We often talk of the Church as a 'body' – some might say it's almost a corpse but that would be uncharitable. A key part of New Testament teaching is that, like a body, the different parts have to accept each other and work together. No one part can say to the others: 'I'm the most important so I don't need you'. It is an inter-dependent community, bound together by a mutual acceptance of their differences; not only a collection of like-minded individuals. 'If the body were all eyes, how would it smell'? Terrible! (Boom. Boom). This is a text that has frequently been totally ignored as various groups have set themselves up as the actual 'true' Church, in contrast to all the rest. It carries on even today, especially among conservative evangelicals or those who refuse to accept the ministry of women. Why else do so many establish new churches rather than throwing in their lot with those that are there already? Many just pick up defecting believers from elsewhere and the body splinters even further.

Surely churches have to be communities that are blurred round the edges and as diverse as possible, not stridently defending 'the' truth as they see it and insisting on everyone signing up to that single path as a condition of entry? That way, in my opinion at least, lies oblivion. I honestly do not think that many churches can survive in our culture, except as a refuge for those are frankly wholly out of step with reality, unless they adapt to our changed and more questioning context. They have to be more 'catholic' and accept a greater range of responses to the questions raised by our existence. If they stick with 'This is true and only we are right', nearly all of us will not want to join in.

We are not going to believe it just because someone else tells us that we should. More and more people are simply not interested in or attracted by such claims and we will increasingly leave religion behind in our search for a more enlightened humanity and new kinds of spirituality. This kind of self-interest group is not the kind of model that many thinking enquirers will find attractive. It is a relatively recent idea that the Christian community includes only those who have made a 'commitment' and is open to 'members only'. Despite my own non-conformist past, where this approach has tended to be the emphasis, I now find the idea of more openness and far less certainty to be much more creative, as well as being much more honest.

After the very early days, Christianity was not largely spread by individual conversions. That would never account for its rapid growth. It became a by-product of empire once the Romans became more tolerant, (though it was probably never the official religion as some have claimed). But a more integrated religion seeking to make some real difference to its wider society has to be very different from a small group intent only on its own common needs. Considerable compromises are required, but in return, far more people get to be part of it and the Church gains greater influence. This was the trade-off that institutional western Christianity chose to accept once Emperor Constantine signalled his changed attitude towards it. Its expansion into the modern world outside Europe is also explained in much the same way. It 'worked', though whether Jesus of Nazareth would recognise it as anything to do with him is an entirely different question.

Again, this all just illustrates the human nature of the whole enterprise. What it meant to be 'a Christian' was very different when whole nations were 'converted' because their king or leader embraced it. Entire families and tribes were now included, but not because they each made an individual decision. It had much more to do with boosting the numbers than any genuine engagement with issues of life and faith. This overlap between Church and nation suited the Church's leaders very well, but it also had its downside for those who dissented from the majority view. Now the Christians were in danger of becoming the oppressors. Until about 150 years ago there was virtually no alternative to being at least a nominal member of the

C of E if you wanted to go to University in this country. Even Baptists and Roman Catholics were barred, (as well as women and Jews). What glorious days these were!

Certain businesses had a religious 'test' before you could work there or the boss would check whether you came to church as a condition of you keeping the job. Being seen in the pew on a Sunday at least now and again was effectively part of the contract. No doubt people just played along with it because they had no choice, but it also meant that religion became a part of people's social identity. It may have had little or nothing to do with what they actually believed but it gave their lives added security. Weddings and funerals might still be the choice of those who never go near a church normally, though both have been losing ground now there are humanist alternatives. How many 'Church' schools contain only actual believers? In rural areas there may be no choice. But it's no secret that some parents and their children are only there, or even at church, because it's a passport to what they see as a better school, now or later. In urban areas many only survive by admitting those of other faiths. But no-one should fool themselves that all this activity is specifically 'Christian', any more than it was in the past.

It's all a bit of a mess, but perhaps that's better than the walls being so well-defined that it's hard to get in. In practice, churches tend to want it both ways. When there's a Queen or King to be crowned, a war to be remembered, a Royal Wedding or state funeral to be held, the whole nation suddenly becomes the focus. The Church relishes its role at the centre of things, and the influence that still goes with it. Bishops in the House of Lords, prayers before each Commons sitting; Army chaplains; hospital chaplains etc. Suddenly we're all included. The doors are thrown open to those who probably don't believe a word of it at any other time. Church and state become virtually indistinguishable; everyone is welcome and little is demanded in return. There is no expectation that everyone must actually believe anything before they can join in. And quite right too.

But at other times churches and Church leaders seem to want to separate themselves and expect the rest of us to fit entirely into their agenda rather than them fitting into ours. Some of the arguments against assisted suicide or abortion, for example, are not much more than an expectation that everyone must behave in a certain way because the religious insight trumps all others. Claiming life is 'sacred' at this point doesn't however always seem to lead to a similar view in other contexts. Opposition to abortion but support for gun ownership and the death penalty among the USA evangelical community is a classic case. At a somewhat more trivial level is the ridiculous argument that the Archbishop of York picked with the National Trust about Easter eggs. He objected to the fact that the publicity didn't focus on the specifically Christian meaning of the word but on bunnies and chocolate. But 'Eostre' is the name of the pagan goddess of Spring. The word doesn't actually belong to the Christians at all. They stole it!

Sometimes, unless you know Jesus 'personally', or much better still, don't know him yet but would like to because your life is such a disaster, you cannot hope to be accepted with values of a different kind. It seems to me that many Christian churches have become their own worst enemies. They have become so focused on 'getting people in' on their terms that perhaps they have failed to see that we are already there! We are all members of the same human race with convictions, values and principles – are churches the only place where good can flourish? Shouldn't they be places where we can all be at our best, at least if some other religion hasn't claimed us first? But so much of what goes on is either unspeakably dull or mind-numbingly crass and superficial. Or I simply cannot share the outdated moral requirements that seem to be expected.

But the biggest problem for me, and I suspect for most people, is still the beliefs; the doctrines. It's what I am asked to affirm as true, formally or informally, that keeps me away. The creeds, of all kinds. But I admit I still rather miss the sense of community, even after all these years, though many others find it in the pub or golf club. The older I get, the more I see that being part of something helps to stave off the loss of a working identity and the feeling of value that came with it. The only local church I feel I can attend is one that has an open table and a very diverse congregation. It welcomes you just on the basis that you want to be part of it. I don't have to say the liturgy; sometimes I just watch and reflect or light a candle. Its language about God is generally inclusive. Some statements of 'faith' I can share in; some I can't, but the Eucharist is offered either way. It gives me a chance to 'remember' Jesus, which is where it all began. Perhaps that is actually enough to belong and we can let go of all the rest.

So at this point on my pilgrimage, as I approach a kind of ending, I am in search of churches that are not so focused on their admission requirements but which can provide a model of a shared humanity. Places where we can have a genuine debate, not a one-sided conversation in which I have to do all the listening. Where theological differences are valued and spiritual innovation welcomed. Can the Christians come up with this, or do I need to look elsewhere? I recognise that this is a big ask, though I suspect that many people in 'ordinary' churches up and down the land are not necessarily there for the deep theology or because they really have a personal relationship with Jesus or are entranced by the reality of God in their lives. Their feelings about the vicar, or the choir, or how warm it is are probably just as, if not more, important. It may just be a habit. That all still has value.

It would easy to be cynical about this, but I accept that they are still finding something worthwhile. The people there are entitled to my respect, as long as they can also accept me as an equal human being without me having to pretend or just fit in. My worry is that so much orthodoxy seems to lead in the opposite direction; to set us against each other not to explore what we have in common. There are undoubtedly some genuine 'saints' out there, most of whom wouldn't recognise the label. Most churches have a long tradition of philanthropy; schools, hospitals and so on, though that largely reflects the fact that Church and state were virtually the same until relatively recently. Much good work still goes on, if sometimes from a religious motivation that can suggest a slightly hidden agenda. I have long been frustrated by those who looked down on the 'social gospel', as if making a difference in the world is somehow not part of their God's 'real' intentions.

Some of this activity is still the promotion of particular moral standards that 'the world' is seen to be eroding. I am more impressed by those who are willing to lose themselves in selfless work with those on the margins, often for little or no reward. In some areas it is virtually only the churches that remain to provide the sort of safety-net that the state no longer provides. They may open for the homeless or befriend the lonely, the asylum-seeker and refugee. We ought to be thoroughly ashamed to see people carrying food parcels for distribution to poorer families as they go into church on a Sunday morning. Changes to benefits suggest that we will need even more of this in future so churches clearly still have their uses.

There are, of course, plenty of 'saints' in other places too. 'Childline' couldn't operate without volunteers. Neither would your local hospice or air ambulance be there when you needed it without those who give their time for free. We still do voluntary work in huge numbers. The 'Big Society' may well have been an empty political gesture designed to cover up the loss of properly-funded local services, but as a description of millions of people's involvement in the mutual care of others it has some merit. Many of these good people no longer feel they can find a place in any church. Many would say their time is better spent in doing something more useful instead and I wouldn't argue with them. All I ask from those who do still see the traditional church as a place they want to be, is an understanding that we are all co-travellers on the same journey, not that some people own the only accurate map and the rest of us are hopelessly lost without it. It is actually all about the kind of people we are and the way we live; that is all that matters

The Church, as its history surely shows, has little to be superior about. A touch of modesty here; an openness to new thinking there; an acceptance that your sexuality or your marital status is not necessarily the most important thing about you as a person; that's all some people want. People who will listen and discuss, not just preach at you. Pulling up the drawbridge and keeping the faithful safe inside just makes us feel like attacking you!

Others start from somewhere else but people like me primarily want to be encouraged to <u>think</u> for ourselves, not to be treated only as an empty vessel into which the 'real' truth can be poured. I have something to contribute to this process. I am a unique human individual, not a problem for you to solve. I don't want to be spoon-fed, patronised or told what I ought to believe or do. I am a grown-up. I have put away the things of childhood so don't treat me like one. Perhaps we can still help each other to be fully human and to find a kind of sainthood together. Our mutual sense of community can be a blessing to the world. This much I believe.

PART 2

'NOT YOUR USUAL SERMON'

Reflections on the Way of Jesus

RETELLING THE STORY

These reflections first appeared as a resource available to download from my website, **www.ben-whitney.org. uk**. They are based on the Common Lectionary passages for 10 Sundays following Pentecost 2019, especially the selected verses from the Gospel of Luke. I hope they will assist those who find difficulty in believing the traditional Christian doctrines and also demonstrate that there is still something in the Jesus story that <u>can</u> be believed and, more importantly, acted upon, with integrity. They are essentially a response to what I call the 'Jesus manifesto' in Luke 4 vv. 18-19, where he is remembered as quoting from Isaiah. What does it mean to preach his 'good news' in the context of the C21st rather than the C1st?

Luke 'the physician' is mentioned by Paul as one of his companions so he was presumed to be the author of two New Testament books, based mainly on the 'we' passages in Acts. We don't know for sure. All the gospels were written after Paul's letters, probably after his death. Most scholars date this gospel to the 70sCE, though some say rather later, with Acts following on sometime after. It seems that Luke had Mark's gospel available to him, plus a source of his own (? written or oral) and, some argue, a shared source with Matthew. It was written in Greek, somewhere in the Mediterranean world, using a

Greek version of the Old Testament for reference, not the original Hebrew.

The dedication to 'Theophilus' (friend of God) is probably a generic title, not an individual. It suggests Luke was writing for a largely non-Jewish audience, sympathetic to new Jesus movement. Despite the author's claim of historical authenticity, all the gospels are not merely writing an objective biography based on known recorded facts. This is Luke's <u>version</u> of Jesus, not <u>the</u> Jesus. The gospels are attempts to explain his significance, not newspaper reports passed on from the time. They each have their own message to tell. Luke and Matthew added to Mark, for example, with the clearly legendary birth stories, in order to push back the Jesus story from his baptism. John is very different and has to be approached with an entirely non-literal attitude. John's Jesus is a mystical, even cosmic creation of the writer; a fascinating insight, not into Jesus himself, but into the beliefs of John's community about him, getting on for 70 years later.

But to see any of the gospels as recording the actual events/words of Jesus would require: (a) that someone remembered/wrote them down at the time, even when we are told that Jesus was alone; (b) that they were passed on without change over two generations or more; (c) that they were then translated accurately from Hebrew/Aramaic into Greek, and (d) that the authors then recorded them in exactly the same format as before, decades after the event. This is all highly improbable.

We don't have any evidence of the existence of any such primary sources. We don't have any original manuscripts or 'first' editions of the gospels, only later copies and translations. I see the gospels, and my use of them, as like Jewish *midrash*: a development of and commentary on the inherited tradition, not its mere repetition. The authors/editors changed what they inherited to make it say something new, relevant to their own context. That is essential to understanding them. This is the only possible explanation for the fact that they don't all agree with each other on many of the details.

So Luke, like the other gospel writers, has written what he sees as the <u>meaning</u> of Jesus' life and teaching, not necessarily what Jesus himself actually did and said at the time. Is this a problem? Not if we see him as storyteller or artist rather than as a historian. He paints a portrait of Jesus; it is not like a photograph or a tape-recording. I have to accept that this is as close as we can get. This is difficult for modern minds but it was common in the ancient world to write in this way 'Literal' truth is not the only kind of truth. So we must always ask 'What is Luke saying about Jesus here'? Not only 'What is Jesus saying here'? That actually helps in applying the text to our times today; it's already an interpretation, not a mere repetition.

I don't write only about the gospel passages in these reflections, even though following the Way of Jesus is my primary focus. I also reflect on the other readings, if often mainly to draw out the back-story to what Luke is writing about or to see what the later Church did with him. I do not see the Bible, or any conclusion from Christian history, as definitive, only as a starting-point. We have learned a lot more since. The past matters. But we read it to understand more about the 'then' and then to reflect on what that means for us, not simply to direct us in the 'now'. We are pilgrims on a journey and some things, even quite precious things, may have to be left behind because they are not worth carrying. They only hold us back from discovering what lies ahead.

PENTECOST SUNDAY
June 9th 2019
Genesis 11: 1-9   Acts 2: 1-21   John 14: 8-17 and 25-27
Psalm 104: 25-35 and 37

MIND THE GAP

A while ago I was at a 'Free to Believe' Conference. (More at **www.freetobelieve.org.uk** if you don't already know about this liberal and inclusive network). We were having lively discussions about Jesus, faith, life and what we each meant by 'God'. In another room, by a considerable contrast, some church group was endlessly praying, weeping, shouting, falling to the floor and singing in tongues etc. The children present looked positively frightened. It went on for hours. Is that what a healthy Christian life lived in the 'Spirit of God' looks like? Not for me certainly. It just sets them apart from everyone else and I have absolutely no desire to be like that.

The Pentecost story is certainly about empowerment, but by whom, how, and for what? Luke's version of how the Spirit came is only one of the recorded ways of how the first followers of Jesus began to share what they believed about him. (See for e.g. John 20:22 and the additional ending to Mark 16). It may have been part of each individual's resurrection experience, whenever that happened, not separated out into stages weeks apart. We are used to the regular liturgical pattern but *every* account of the life, death, teaching and resurrection of Jesus is a version 'according to' someone, or some community, not *the* version. They're not all the same.

Pentecost was a Jewish celebration day: Shavuot; a 24 hour vigil 50 days after Passover, celebrating the giving of the Law to Moses. According to Luke, people from all over the known world were gathered in Jerusalem. It's a multi-national jamboree. This is the setting in which this writer chooses to launch his story of the early church though it seems, like other NT writers, he thought that these were the 'last days' as well as the first.

And what is the experience he describes? Unlike Paul elsewhere, nothing to do with ecstatic utterances or semi-trance-like states, (neither of which are uniquely Christian experiences anyway), but the words of Peter heard 'in our own language'. Actual spoken languages; the equivalent of French or German today. What is Luke saying, given that he is writing for a largely Gentile audience? This Spirit is for every nation; it transcends all human boundaries and cultures. It was always meant to be so. The Jews should have realised it wasn't just for them. He has Peter quote the prophet Joel:

In the last days it will be, God declares, that I will pour out my Spirit upon all flesh, and your sons and your daughters shall prophesy, and your young men shall see visions, and your old men shall dream dreams. (Joel 2:28)

Unfortunately Luke also seems to suggest that only the disciples actually had this experience directly, which rather misses his own point! But in contrast to the way John also has Jesus talking about the 'Comforter or Counsellor' for the believers only in 14:16 and 26, this offer of the Spirit is for 'all flesh', or in the Psalm, 'the whole earth'.

Presumably this includes everyone, or was all this now only for the followers of Jesus? To claim so suggests that we are in control of it, not that it is freely available to all. This particular version of the Spirit's coming puts right what the ancient story of Babel in Genesis 11 had outlined as the problem with all humanity. We just don't talk to, or listen to, each other. It's a dialogue of the deaf most of the time. The Jews had forgotten they were supposed to be a 'light to the nations', not a self-saving sect. Jesus' Way offers a different dimension, not just another exclusive group who think that they alone have all the answers.

Why were there so many divisions between people? Why are there still? In these stories, language acts as a symbol for why there are often great gaps between us. When you can't understand what others are saying, and they can't understand you, our ability to co-operate and respect each other is undermined. The coming of the Spirit in the way that Luke describes it challenges all our prejudices about seemingly unavoidable distinctions of race and nationhood, and, in modern contexts, religion, gender, sexuality, class, culture, etc. This Spirit unites; it does not divide.

If you look at Church history you could be forgiven for thinking the opposite, given the splits, separations and sects that have happened over the years. But unity, if with considerable diversity, is the only way forward, in life or in the Church. Christians must surely challenge those who try to put the gaps back in again by calling for more emphasis on ourselves, our own nation or our own religion first; people like us. There is no 'us' and 'them' anymore. Just one common humanity, where each person is equally important.

We have to speak in a C21st century language about all this; one that fits with what people know to be true in the rest of their lives and enables them to hear what we are saying. So not so much a gift, I would say, as a discovery: an insight into what helps us to be fully human. Which brings us to a very fundamental underlying issue. Do we have to attribute this activity to a 'God' as the only way to bring about this renewing and creative thing among us?

It's a big question but one that is rarely asked, just assumed. If we can't find a vocabulary that works in the modern world no-one will take any notice. Why should they? So much of what the Church says sounds so exclusive, not inclusive. An experience for us 'in here'; not a transformation of life 'out there'. You have to believe what we believe to receive it. The claims are based only on what we have already decided is 'true' – and most people don't share the same assumptions.

We can only ever talk about God in human terms. I believe we need to think far less of 'a' supernatural Being, (a bit like us only bigger) and much more, if we still use the word at all, as a dimension of ourselves. More of an adjective or adverb than a noun. The sum of all *our* hopes, ideals and values, not an external object or Person. 'Godness' is found when we encounter our deepest self, individually and together.

We may even say, as the NT writers did, that 'God is Love' to express the significance of that inherently *human* value, and leave it at that. Jesus used the term 'Father', as we may do, but that is also a simile or metaphor, not a statement about biology or reproduction, couched in language that made sense at the time. A comparison, if a rather patriarchal one, from our own experience. 'Like a father', (or indeed a mother).

So what then can we still say about this 'Holy Spirit' that sustains us, including, but not only, those who walk in the Way of Jesus? '*The* Holy Spirit' implies so much that is not here in this story. I prefer to use the phrase, 'a spirit of holiness' to describe how we can now relate to this idea of an empowering and enabling life that moves within us, as it did in Jesus. We have devised a range of images and comparisons to express this sense of creative energy; wind, fire, spark, breath. They are there in both the Old and the New Testaments if you look for them. The '*ruach*' (feminine in Hebrew) breathes through us but cannot be known, defined or contained.

At our best, we can find the power to be all that we seek to be. To be 'holy' is to be 'human'. This quest for true fulfilment offers us hopes and dreams; it gives us visions of how things could be, not a judgemental despair at how things are. It gives us an ability to read the signs of the times and make prophetic statements that help to bring about positive change, in us and in the world.

This has nothing at all to do with being superior over others in worship or in life. That is mere self-indulgence. But wherever humanity is enhanced, good is done, prejudices overcome, relationships restored, barriers broken down; there a spirit of holiness can be found. It is as if we are in tune with the unifying heartbeat of the Universe; its breath lives in our breath. We are brought closer to the more excellent ways of love and peace. We can find both a personal and communal healing as this spirit of holiness fills the gaps and divisions between us. According to the Christian story, it's all down to us now. So we had better get on with it!

SECOND SUNDAY AFTER PENTECOST
June 23rd 2019
Isaiah 65: 1-9   Galatians 3: 23-29   Luke 8: 26-39
Psalm 22: 18-27

LETTING GO OF 'GOD'

(I've passed on Trinity Sunday for obvious reasons, but see Chapter 3).

The radical follower of the Way of Jesus is not necessarily a 'Christian'. Christianity is a set of doctrines and claims that have been devised by us, mostly in centuries past. But 'it ain't necessarily so'. Jesus didn't write the Creeds, or the letters of Paul. It is difficult for us to think ourselves back into a culture where the existence of a supernatural 'God' was just taken for granted and the only issue at stake was whether or not the people were obedient to 'His' ways.

This is the concern confronting the writer of our OT passage, putting his own words into his God's mouth. God is desperate to reach out to the people, (one of several anthropomorphic metaphors in this reading where 'God' is given very human characteristics). But the people take no notice or are deliberately going against 'His' instructions. This is not a criticism of those who do not claim to follow the religious path but of those who do. Their actions and observances are pointless. All their incense and sacrifices mean nothing.

You may have noticed all the inverted commas above. I won't always bother in future, but here I just want to remind us that any language about 'God' is only that; just words, not an actual description. 'God' is a name we may give to whatever we conceive of as the basis of our humanity, not 'His' actual name. You may not even use the word at all and speak only of human experience and the mystery beyond, because anything else is unknowable. Religious language may claim to be more than this but it is not. Any 'religious' activity, 'revelation' or event is *always* a human activity, idea or experience that we choose to label as 'religious'. It cannot be anything else.

'If horses could paint their gods they would look like horses' – attributed to Xenophanes 2500 years ago. We can never step away from the boundaries of our humanity. The images are all our own, limited by our human perceptions. These ideas then become mere idols if we treat them as 'God'. So nothing cannot be questioned, discussed, revised or renewed. Nothing is a 'given' from on high.

Isaiah's 'God' is actually more in tune with those who do *not* claim allegiance to 'Him': '*I was ready to be sought out by those who did not ask; to be found by those who did not seek me*' not those who claim to be more 'religious' than everyone else. They are *'a smoke in my nostrils, a fire that burns all day long'.*

Unlike for the people in the time of Isaiah, our historic images of God no longer count for much outside the Church. Most people in our culture have decided, correctly, that the old 'God' who controls everything that happens is unbelievable. As Anthony Freeman wrote in *'God in Us'*, that may be the most important step that anyone can take in order to find a more genuine and living faith. Those who do believe, as usually defined, can no longer assume that it is all entirely obvious and that those who do not believe as they do are just being perverse and disobedient.

Those on the outside may actually have something important to tell those on the inside. Our words and our claims about a 'God' mean nothing to them simply because we keep repeating them or calling on His name. If 'God' is especially there for those who are not looking for Him, the beliefs of those who think they have found Him may even be getting in the way. The gospel writers suggest Jesus made similar points about those who thought they were 'saved' but weren't and those who were but didn't realise it. Once you think you have found it, you have lost it.

I am sure that Paul never meant his own words to become as prescriptive as the Church has made them. But it could be argued that he 'invented' Christianity out of the story of Jesus, which was actually about something else entirely. He was primarily trying to sort out the problems in the disparate communities that he cared about in what he believed to be the short time remaining before it all came to an end, not laying down requirements for centuries to come. For all his emphasis elsewhere on the exclusivity of faith, he writes in the Galatians passage of the liberation that believing should bring. It is not about adhering to 'law'. Human distinctions and categorisations are irrelevant. It's not about conforming to one set way of believing or deciding who's in and who's out. It's much more about being 'like Jesus' as best we can.

Our gospel passages will return time and time again to the remembered emphasis on Jesus' welcome to those seen as outsiders. The setting for Luke's story about the madman and the pigs is beyond the Jewish territory; across the lake of Galilee. Jesus seems to have often gone there. I always feel rather sorry for whoever owned the pigs; that's their livelihood gone. Thanks very much Jesus! But the man who was healed is told to stay put, outside the mainstream and talk about what has happened to him there, not to abandon his own community.

There is no invitation to join Jesus' band of followers and go back with him but a call to be a source of hope and encouragement where he is. I hear so much talk in the Church of 'taking the message out' to those who do not already know it. We devise mission strategies and plans; publish endless booklets and constantly exhort the faithful. And what is the message? It's all about 'getting people in', and entirely on our terms. Posters outside invite motorists to come and find the truth about life and death. 'Jesus is the answer', (maybe, but what is the question?) 'Come on an Alpha course'. It's the same old wine, just in recycled wineskins; not anything genuinely new for our time.

I wonder if we need to put things entirely the other way around? Maybe we should be letting go of what we think is so precious, even our idea of God, and listening, not talking at all. Encouraging people to stay where they are, not to come in here where all the answers are supposedly to be found. If the customers aren't buying what we have to sell, maybe the problem is with us, and with the product, not with them.

It's all very warm and comforting to be part of a congregation where everyone feels secure and confident; to go away from worship affirmed in your faith and reassured that you are on the right track. I enjoy the aesthetic experience of cathedral services, always professionally and expertly done. My senses are stimulated and my spirts are lifted. But maybe it's still all getting up God's nose because we are focusing so much on ourselves.

The Psalms tend to reinforce this need for reassurance. The writer of Psalm 22 asks for God not to be far away and promises to worship Him in return. Perhaps most people have abandoned the God who means so much to the believers because they do not share the basis of this contract. This God who will always look after you because you are special to Him is not real for them. Human experience tells them it's not true.

They don't necessarily want to be part of some chosen elite; certainly not at the expense of others. This is the God who is as good as dead since Nietzsche and that's no bad thing. That God is merely a tribal totem; always looking out for *us*, but not the source of life for *all* humanity, whatever our religion or creed; or even if we have chosen not to follow one at all but just to live life to the full and hurt no-one else along the way.

It may be tempting to think otherwise but perhaps I should be feeling unsettled, insecure and challenged after attending church. Made to question, not reassured. Encouraged to let go of 'God', not to hold on. Made to think about something from outside my comfort zone. The real emphasis should be on what is happening out there, not in here. Psalm 22 also recognises that the end product of all this worship is that the poor will eat and be satisfied. Time in church should lead to action, and mostly among those who weren't there. Otherwise we can't expect what we've been doing to have any real spiritual value for us or anyone else, no matter how much we hope our 'God' will notice.

THIRD SUNDAY AFTER PENTECOST
June 30th 2019
1 Kings 19:15-16 and 19-21   Galatians 5:1 and 13-25
Luke 9: 51-62   Psalm 16

FREEDOM TO BELIEVE

The history of the Christian Church is strong on continuity; the present must be consistent with the past it is often said. Following on from examples in the Old Testament like Moses and Aaron, Elijah and Elisha, there's been an emphasis on handing on the truth, not on re-inventing it. Aaron fulfils Moses' mission, he doesn't start a new one. Elisha picks up Elijah's mantle and carries on as he did. The Popes and even C of E bishops are all allegedly in a continuous line of apostolic succession from Peter, even though we know that such an idea has hardly a grain of historical truth. Many Popes got there by imprisoning potential rivals, or even worse. The motives of Henry VIII in breaking from Rome cannot surely be seen as primarily driven by a search for a more authentic Church in line with Jesus and the first Christians!

Few Christians seem willing to say that what was believed in the past was wrong and it's time for something different. So is it the Church's job to keep the ancient flame alive? To keep calling people back to the basics that were defined hundreds of years ago. Or are there times when we need to light an entirely new candle that burns in a very different way to light up a very different world? Or is the continuity of faith like the gardener who's used the same brush for 40 years, even though it's had 2 new handles and 3 new heads in the meantime?

Change is never easy. William of Ockham (1321), an English philosopher and theologian in late medieval Europe, said 'our faith is not formed by the wisdom of the Pope' and so no-one was bound to believe him in matters of faith. That was dynamite! Martin Luther's views were just as outrageous to the Church hierarchy later. Should we now see Don Cupitt or John Shelby Spong in the same light? Perhaps the future will. What does each person (including the clergy) actually *mean* when they say the words of the Creed? How do we know? I suspect that most ideas are pretty vague, or we would find considerable variety. But is that necessarily a bad thing? The Psalmist says his own 'heart' teaches him. We are each have to find our own way, not just copy someone else's.

Paul writes here of the importance of freedom. I sometimes think that many of the more 'evangelical' approaches foster a kind of modern slavery. One such church I know has a statement of required faith on its website that runs to hundreds of words and defines in minute detail what must be believed to belong. It reads like a complex test that has to be revised for and passed first. There is no room for individual interpretation or innovation it seems, unless it comes from those already in charge. This church also prevents women from occupying any position of leadership and 'permits' them only be involved in teaching other women and children, not men. (Hello! It's the C21st!) It is popular with young professionals. I really don't understand why, though I gather some do leave after a while because the restrictions become too great.

The Church used to support actual slavery – so it *can* change its mind about things and what it believes to be right – but this strikes me as an intellectual and spiritual equivalent, despite its apparent popularity for some. Ultimately it seems to be all about exercising power, which has no place among us, at least as was remembered about Jesus and his way of leading and inspiring others.

It's interesting that Paul's summary of the law doesn't mention God! But it could be argued that he then ignores his own advice by laying down a lot of prescriptive rules. It wouldn't be the only example where a commitment to freedom is conditional on us using that freedom only as someone else allows. I prefer to read him as recognising those ways of living that in the end bind and restrict us, even if they may seem very liberating and attractive at the time, and those that actually set us free to live in community with one another and at peace with ourselves.

I do not see, for example, why so many religious people seem so hung up on same-sex relationships, even to the point of excluding those who are in them from participating in church life or taking up positions of leadership. But that is not to say I would advocate promiscuity, by anyone of any sexuality, because that seems to me to lead to a general unhappiness and is not good for us. I am content, I think like Paul, to make a distinction between 'freedom' to explore your own path without permission from anyone else, and 'license' to do whatever you like.

In seeking to restrict the former, we may even be encouraging the latter by denying people caring and supportive contexts in which to be themselves. Ultimately, Paul says, those who seek to bite others may get bitten in return. How many of those taking the hardest line about what other people must believe or the way that they must behave, end up failing to meet their own requirements and suffer emotional and spiritual breakdowns as a result? (Like St. Augustine or maybe even Paul himself). Dealing with our supposed guilt and inevitable failure takes over, not life in all its fullness. Faith should give us wings, not a straitjacket.

In another of Luke's stories about Jesus and outsiders, he writes that the rather suspicious Samaritans chose not to follow his Way and ignored him. James and John were all for immediate retribution in response to their decision, but Jesus rebukes, not the Samaritans, but his disciples. Others appeared more willing but the obstacles were too great. Luke has Jesus talking about the insecurity created by his offer and he seems to at least understand the reasons for their reluctance. There is certainly no suggestion of force or power being involved as James and John seem to think they should be.

People are free to reject the Way of Jesus. My worry is that we so often simply offer them a rehashed version of ideas inherited from Christian history, not a genuine encounter with the human person he really was before all that was invented. Jesus has been portrayed as emperor, king, judge, master; all images of male power totally unrelated to what we can discern about him from what we know of his remembered teaching. Pictures on ancient Cathedral walls had him arriving from the sky sending the faithless to endless torment, and the faithful to what looks like a pretty boring eternity standing about waiting for something to happen. That's not what he means to me. He did not have a halo, did not know the future in advance and had the same human feelings as we do. Do we actually tell our contemporaries the truth about who Jesus was so that they can make an informed choice?

Jesus was human, not superhuman. Neither does our concept of God have to be seen in the traditional way. It is hard to find other words to use but if we don't even try, the god that we have made in our own image will simply be rejected as belonging to another age. If we haven't revised our ideas in the light of Darwin and what we now know about the Universe, no wonder others see us as living in a religious ghetto unrelated to real life. The beliefs that we have created can so easily be repeated only because we think that's what we still have to say. They may not be what actually needs saying in our time and place in order to make faith live.

So what should our freedom to believe look like? A new, more humanist focus can open up new understandings of what it means to still seek a 'spiritual' way of living. New liturgies can be far more inclusive than before, avoiding all the unnecessary male terms when talking of God. New songs can move our thoughts onto ways of caring for the world, not just reassuring ourselves or keeping God happy by praising 'Him' all the time. We can celebrate our diversity in lifestyle and belief, not be embarrassed to admit it and expect everyone to toe the party line.

The past isn't always the best guide. So imagine if our Creeds started with: '*We have let go of everything we thought we knew and this is what Jesus actually means for us, here and now*', said without fear of criticism because you don't reach the same conclusions as before. I wonder where that would lead? Perhaps to renewal!

FOURTH SUNDAY AFTER PENTECOST
July 7th 2019
Isaiah 66: 10-14   Galatians 6: 1-16   Luke 10:1-11
and 16-20   Psalm 66: 1-8

IS THE BIBLE TRUE?

The cover of my Bible says 'Holy' Bible. I wish it didn't. I don't worship it. One of the constant challenges for those who are not comfortable with the usual formulations of what it means to be a 'Christian' is how we should approach it. The set passages are my starting point, but I don't feel I always have to simply repeat what they say as beyond all discussion and debate. I bring something to this encounter that the writers didn't know about. Many understandings of faith do seem to presuppose that we are still stuck in a C1stCE world, or even older, and so we must still see things now as they did then. Why? We don't say that about medicine, or physics or human rights etc.

But everything 'Christian', many say, must fit with what it says in the Bible. So do I always have to find a relevant text to justify every opinion or can I just say and think what I believe to be right in the light of all the knowledge and experience that is available to me now? Who decided that every single word of the Bible was the final authoritative 'Word of God' forever? That claim is not made by any of the classic Creeds. Many have given up trying to walk in the Way of Jesus because they can't square this particular circle. The Church is not a community dedicated to the preservation of old manuscripts; but it can look a bit like that from outside.

Some of those who have rejected the Bible as of any value may, of course, be mistaken and it doesn't necessarily say what they think it says. Or maybe we have failed to use it properly, or to share it with them in meaningful way, by turning it into something 'holy' that it was never meant to be. There can be no denying that it reflects a very different world from ours but once we accept that we don't always have to agree with it and take the Bible down from its pedestal, the *human* story that it tells might still have some resonance.

But there is work for us to do, not merely lazy repetition or selective quotation. We actually have no 'original' manuscripts anyway to rely on; only versions, copies and translations. And they do not always agree with each other. The Bible illuminates our path; it cannot always direct it. And sometimes it really surprises! Isaiah writes, in the name of his God, of the comfort that the people will find in their holy Temple: *As a mother comforts her child, so I will comfort you; you shall be comforted in Jerusalem.*

So, according to 'the Bible', God is like a mother! That makes a change. It can hardly be denied that the Biblical world was deeply patriarchal; almost everything focuses on fathers and sons, with women given mostly walk-on parts here and there or, more accurately, their actual contributions overlooked and downplayed in the retelling, including in the gospels. (This is a particularly 'macho' Psalm!) This can make the whole story feel inaccessible and outdated. Other approaches to understanding the 'Divine' are very much in the minority and you have to look hard for them. But here at least is a useful reminder that God is not male and so we may need other images to counteract the more usual ones. (See for e.g. '*She sits like a bird*'; one of the many hymns by John Bell/ Iona Community that uses feminine images and inclusive language).

So, I wonder, how will those still wedded to the image of God as 'Father' react to 'the Bible' here? They should surely be asked to reflect on other approaches, even if it means going against much that they may have taken for granted. And perhaps this conversation will also bring hope to those who cannot identify with the traditional concept. 'If God is like my father you can keep him' is a genuine obstacle for many and not to be ignored. Jesus talked of God as 'Father'. But 'fatherhood' is not the same as 'maleness'. Some passages about the fatherhood of God include characteristics like care and tenderness that our culture, like Isaiah's, usually associate more with mothers. There is a fluidity of images here that we mustn't force to fit our gender stereotypes.

Paul too surprises me. His words are often used to criticise and even condemn. But the tone is forgiving, not one of condemnation, when someone fails to live up to the expected standard. Imposing your own values on others, (he uses the example of circumcision), is unacceptable. As in 1 Corinthians 12, the body metaphor requires an acceptance of diversity. It is not optional. The 'Biblical' standard is to seek the ways of 'gentleness, peace and mercy'. There is no need to stand in judgement of anyone; just love them.

The Church, by contrast, can often use 'the Bible' to justify being rigid, unforgiving and hyper-critical, especially about issues of personal and social morality. Even if all the individual people there don't actually think in that rather superior way, that's often what it looks like. 'All are welcome at the Lord's table' so why do some churches still make it seem so difficult by always emphasising their own view of 'what the Bible says'? 'The Bible' is actually nothing like so clear-cut as we often assume and much of it is frankly unacceptable to modern minds. It simply cannot be the last word on everything forever. Even those who say it is still pick and choose the bits they like and ignore anything that might say something different; about giving away your wealth, for example.

Jesus was a Jew at a particular time, steeped, as a human being, in the world view and language then available. But there is a very radical edge to his apparent re-interpretation of the Jewish scriptures. He was certainly no fundamentalist! The religious leaders saw him as a heretic and blasphemer; enough to get him crucified. But here also is a reminder of the need to remember that each gospel has an author and a history of how it came to be written, well after the event. To me, this particular passage reads more like a story of Luke's group facing rejection 40 or more years later than as an example of Jesus' own approach to his ministry. We can never be entirely sure. Jesus didn't write it!

Matthew, for example, talks only about Jesus sending out the 12 and the number 70 (or 72) is clearly meant to mean something – the number of all the known Gentile nations in Genesis 10 perhaps or the elders appointed to help Moses in Numbers 11? It is also the number of scholars believed to have produced the Greek version of the Hebrew scriptures, the one used by Luke. The text is full of symbolism, pictures and contradictions, not just 'facts'.

Last week we were reading about Jesus being generous to those who rejected him; now he seems to express their final condemnation. The missing verses in the set passage are a series of curses against whole Galilean towns for their sinfulness, comparing them to Sodom etc. but Jesus himself seems to have been well-received in Capernaum (e.g. 4:32). There are also many mythological elements: Satan's fall from heaven, demons, snakes, scorpions etc. This whole passage makes the rule of God sound like a threat, not a promise. Believe it or else! This is surely the later Church expressing its own frustrations, not the Way of Jesus.

So maybe this is just Luke talking, not Jesus. Let's not be afraid to say that the Bible isn't always to be taken at face-value. Perhaps such an attitude even makes it live as part of our human story, not as something different that came from somewhere else. If you take a responsible approach to the text you can ask questions of it, dig beneath the surface and still come up with a story of people like us from which we can learn. It's not a recipe book, always to be followed to the letter. And anyway, departing from the recipe can bring new and exciting flavours!

Perhaps we should do more to help people to ask out loud something that they might only have thought secretly. 'Is the Bible really true – and what do I mean when I ask that question?' What different kinds of 'truth' are there? A life of faith is not about adhering to any book, writer or idea. It's about each of us being fully human. So what guiding principles do I need, about my understanding of 'God' or about how to live? What does it mean, to paraphrase Paul, not to hold on to *anything* but to Jesus and his dying? Not to any previously precious 'truth' that someone else has told us we cannot change. We face an unknown future, but we have an inspirational fellow-traveller so be ready to be surprised!

FIFTH SUNDAY AFTER PENTECOST
July 14th 2019
Deuteronomy 30: 9-14   Colossians 1: 1-14
Luke 10: 25-37   Psalm 25: 1-9

CARING FOR STRANGERS

'John was usually very cautious at the cash-machine, especially on these damp and gloomy evenings. He always made sure that no-one else could see his PIN and put the money away as quickly as he could. But this time he never even saw the muggers coming before he hit the ground. They took the cash, of course, as well as his wallet and mobile phone. There was no need to kick him while he was down as well, but at least they didn't stab him. He'd have given them what they wanted if they'd just asked for it.

It was quiet in the high street tonight. Not many people about and those that were there were obviously anxious to get home. The vicar was no doubt pre-occupied with prayer after a particularly challenging pastoral visit. The police patrol car didn't even slow down; probably going to some other emergency of greater importance. The doctor's surgery across the road was, inevitably, closed.

It was getting dark now. So John was worried at first when the unlicensed minicab stopped and this young Asian chap got out. Hadn't he suffered enough already? John had never been too keen on 'Pakis' as he called them. What with their foreign ways and their funny food: why didn't they go back where they came from? He was even more surprised when the driver asked him if he was alright, then gently led him to his car and took him to Casualty. He even bought John a cup of tea and stayed with him till his daughter arrived. 'No charge mate', he said, as he left. John never did get his name.'

It's such a timeless story, such a powerful message, and so typical of what we can discern elsewhere about Jesus' teaching, that it is odd that none of the other synoptic gospels included it. The general assumption is that Luke's source had preserved this story but that Mark's and Matthew's sources didn't know about it. Or maybe Luke just wrote it himself to illustrate his understanding of Jesus from a few remembered fragments. No one gospel gives us the whole picture of Jesus and Luke broadens our understanding of his memory with stories like this.

The context within which the story is set is important. Jesus had been asked a question by some smart religious lawyer about what he must do to receive eternal life. Of course he thought he knew the answer to his own question already. Follow the law; keep the commandments and so on. Presumably this was intended as a not very subtle trap for Jesus to fall into and to see how well this so-called teacher knew his stuff.

But, like all good interviewees, Jesus answers the question with another question – 'What do the scriptures say? How do you read them?' The lawyer comes back with the standard formula about loving both God and neighbour. Job done. That's me home and dry. Luke suggests that Jesus didn't get into a discussion about God. 'So love your neighbour then' he says. 'Ah, but who is my neighbour'?

Not quite who he thought it was. The Jews loathed and despised the Samaritans. They were the modern descendants of the renegade tribes which had split from the true nation of God centuries before. Samaritans were outsiders, lesser people, who did not enjoy God's favour and blessing. And it was one of these who Jesus holds up as the example for the lawyer to follow. I bet he went off muttering a few choice non-legal words under his breath!

This is not just a story just about us doing good works, though it is that. Chad Varah, the priest who founded the modern-day Samaritans, set the organisation up because he heard of a young girl who had killed herself because she had started menstruating. Because she didn't understand what was happening to her, she assumed she must be suffering from some dreadful disease and, it seems, she had no-one to turn to for help. So he set up some phone lines and recruited volunteers to be on hand so that there was someone the suicidal and the desperate could turn to.

But there's another dimension to the story that seems to have been Luke's real point. Luke's Jesus challenges all our usual perceptions. This isn't a story about a Jew helping a Samaritan – commendable and exemplary as that would have been for the lawyer to follow. It's a story about a Samaritan helping a Jew; about the alien foreigner being held up as an example. It's even more outrageous that it first appears. It's about breaking down prejudice and recognising that there is goodness to be found in some very unlikely places.

It's about allowing others to do good to us and acknowledging their value, even if they are not 'one of us'. The Psalmist also seems to recognise that truth doesn't belong only to those who think they know better than others: Psalm 25:8 *'He guides the humble in doing right and teaches his way to the lowly'*. The overlooked outsider sets the example to follow.

This is why I get so cross when those who do claim belief in God seem to assume that they are somehow morally superior to those who do not. Many people are sick of being lectured to by 'His' obviously flawed and self-appointed representatives. The faithful might need to learn a lesson from the faithless. It is not enough just to do good to those who are close to us; those like us; those with whom we are already on friendly terms and who would no doubt do the same for us.

The model of the Good Samaritan is that he did good to someone from whom he was estranged and who might not have given him the time of day had the roles been reversed. Would the Jew have stopped for the Samaritan? Would John have cared for the taxi-driver? Would the Christian necessarily stand up for the 'illegal immigrant' or asylum-seeker? Luke's Jesus suggests that they would do it for us. The example being set and the challenge being made is much more than might at first appear.

Is Luke also saying, in his context, that the Gentiles can now come to the rescue of the Jews? (He may have been a non-Jew himself). The OT passage had suggested that God blesses only those who worship him. If we scratch God's back, He'll scratch ours; if we don't, He won't. Luke's Jesus seems to suggest that things have changed – the understanding has moved on. It's one of the radical ways he reinterprets the existing law.

You don't keep the commandments in order to bring about any reward for yourself at all but to show your love for your 'neighbour', (and that means anyone in need). There is nothing in it for me. The *only* test of faith is what difference I make to others. As Paul writes, it's about 'bearing fruit in every good work'. Being enthusiastic in your faith doesn't make you more special spiritually or more deserving of your eventual 'salvation'. Doing good for the benefit of others is just the way we should live, and for its own sake alone. 'To give and not to count the cost' (or indeed the benefit).

As the OT reading also says, it's not about being so heavenly minded we are no earthly use. It's not about complying with a complicated set of distant doctrinal requirements that are difficult to get to and need an expert to interpret in order to keep you in line. It's about being ourselves; the best we can be and bringing hope where it's most needed. What is required is right under your nose and 'written in your heart'. You know what is right. So just do it!

And those who we might think are least like us may have the most to teach us. The follower of another faith. The child. The person with a disability. The atheist! What difference would it make if we spent more time in our services celebrating ways of sharing the essential goodness of our common humanity with others, not castigating ourselves, or others, for our alleged failures? Beliefs, claims and spiritual self-confidence are not the best measure of our personal or corporate wholeness. A life of faith should be focused on what difference it makes to how we live. In contemporary language, it's all about outcomes, not process.

SIXTH SUNDAY AFTER PENTECOST
July 21st 2019
Genesis 18: 1-10a   Colossians 1: 15-28   Luke 10: 38-42
Psalm 15

THE SEARCH FOR HAPPINESS

Does your idea of God include a sense of humour? A difficult question to answer if you have a conventional idea of God as often portrayed. Perhaps an easier one for those like me who see all our talk of God as a projection, based on human experiences and ideas. We're just painting pictures. Then it's entirely reasonable to talk 'as if' God feels things as we do. He too gets angry and sad at the state of things. Even saying that 'God is Love' is attributing to the eternal something that, as far as I can tell, belongs only to the human. So as long as we recognise what we are doing, perhaps there is no problem in saying that God could laugh, as well as weep.

Laughter is part of our humanity; it is good for us so, in that sense it must also be 'Godlike'. There are many Biblical references to joy, in heaven and on earth. 'Heaven invites us to a party'! Psalm 23 talks of life with God being like a banquet, even if that hope seems to relate only to what comes next. (I'd be happy to do the washing up!) We are surely meant to enjoy our life, not to see it only as an oppressive 'vale of tears'.

The compliers of Israel's ancient histories have included just a few stories which might make us smile now and again, alongside all the blood, sacrifice, wars etc. Read on a bit further from the verses included in the OT reading and Sarah certainly thought that God was having a laugh with the suggestion that at her age she would have a son. The joys of sex were well in the past for her, and for Abraham, she thought, chuckling to herself. The rather po-faced narrators thought she was mocking God by making such a response and made her get 'religious' again by v.15. But just for a moment the idea that she might be allowed to enjoy God and 'His' ways holds sway. (For more examples of creative thinking on this story and others see 'Sarah laughed: Women's voices in the Old Testament' by Trevor Dennis. SPCK 2010)

Luke tells us the story of two sisters that also makes me smile. I hate to contradict his Jesus but I'm not sure that Martha wasn't the one with the more important role of the two. I wonder how the conversation between them went after he had left. I know enough about marriage and family life to know that disputes over who does the housework can begin in a light-hearted way but soon become a serious business. It's a short step from the calm waters of gentle irony to the shark-infested seas of hostile sarcasm! Was Jesus perhaps only making a gentle joke among close friends, not issuing a searing criticism?

Humour can, of course, also have a cutting edge. Paul in 1 Cor.1:23 talks of how the death of Jesus is an obstacle for the Jews but a joke to the Gentiles. But what seems like foolishness is actually wisdom. The musical 'Godspell' portrayed Jesus as a clown. As in Shakespeare the fool sees what others do not. The court jester was allowed to criticise the king or queen. It's a long tradition. Jesus says what others dare not say; he sees what is really going on and isn't afraid to say so. Humour can cut through hypocrisy and make us think.

So, to return to my original question, in this passage Paul writes that Jesus is the 'image of the invisible God'. (He is not saying that Jesus *was* God so that's as far as we need to go in my opinion). God is like Jesus was. Forgiving. Radical. Different from current religious ideas. And humour certainly seems to have played a part in Jesus' teaching style – planks and splinters, camels and eyes of needles, for example. (This second example is probably a reference to a mistranslated Aramaic word into Greek that originally meant a thick ship's rope – though a camel is funnier).

There is no actual reference to Jesus laughing, as far as I am aware, as there is to him weeping. The memories were perhaps too painful for that. There are, however, plenty of examples of Jesus relaxing, eating meals and spending time with his friends. They must have been occasions filled with laughter if they were anything like the meals that we share with one another. I was told by the temperance lady when I was a child that the wine Jesus drank definitely wasn't alcoholic! I beg to differ. Indeed it seems that he and his disciples had a reputation for enjoying themselves a bit too much and even being drunkards and gluttons. Going about the Father's business doesn't mean never enjoying yourself.

His yoke is 'easy'; well sometimes. Perhaps this Sunday, at the start of most people's holiday season, is a good time to ask whether we place enough emphasis on enjoying our lives as followers of Jesus. Of course it can mean conflict and struggle (see August 18th) but maybe we also need to relax a little more and not feel guilty for doing so. Joy is part of our humanity to be celebrated, not to be ashamed of. Happiness is a hoped-for, if elusive, human goal for everyone.

One of the ways of translating the Beatitudes in Matthew 5 and Luke 6, for example, is to use the word 'happy' instead of 'blessed' for those who live in the ways that Jesus suggests. Again it's not known what he actually said, especially as there are two versions, but being 'blessed' implies to me that this behaviour will result in a reward only later. Saying 'happy' are the poor etc. suggests that the joy comes now. If these transformations are to come about, including from weeping to laughter, *we* have to make it happen, for ourselves and for one another, not just wait for some compensation after we've died. Perhaps there's a mixture of both ideas in the different writers' minds.

Neil Baldwin, the former Stoke City kit man whose life was made into the film, '*Marvellous*', said he made up his mind to be happy and then he was. But he also received much love and care from others along the way. Cognitive Behavioural Therapy helps people to do much the same – to think themselves happy by looking at life's events in a different way. 'Don't worry; be happy'. Maybe Jesus got there first!

What does the church have to offer those looking for genuine happiness? Not merely the superficiality of jolly spiritual entertainment (God Allmatey!) and escapist optimism. Sometimes it looks like that's the focus. Paul might disagree with me but I'm not at all sure either that real happiness comes from a certainty in our own salvation. Maybe that's closer to smug; not an attractive human quality. But is there a real sense of community that sustains those going through hard times? Genuine companionship with others on the journey?

True happiness for ourselves comes from playing our part in making other people happy; it's an incidental spin-off, not why we do it. We have something different to say from the messages peddled in the Sunday supplements, the glossy magazines and on social media about what brings us true well-being. It's not about being rich and famous or being the star of your own YouTube or Instagram show. It's not about the clothes you wear, the car you drive or owning the latest phone. The 'me generation' is a caricature but there is some truth in it. Maybe the 'selfie' should be seen as a symbol for a way of living that is bound to disappoint. Many end up realising they don't look half as good as they think they do; or are desperate for the 'likes' they never get. This inevitable disappointment can have devastating effects.

Seeking only our own happiness is not the main reason why we are on this journey with Jesus. The often sad ending can't be avoided; loss and its consequent grief is an ever-present reality. Perhaps we never really get over the shock of being born and leaving our mother's womb. It's as if we are always striving to find the security we once had. Some people never seem to let themselves relax and simply have fun. But we are allowed to be affirmed as valuable human beings along the way, and that's a good feeling, as long as we are laughing with others, not about them behind their backs. The Way of Jesus is not one long picnic. But it's not all fasting and flagellation either.

So what's the only reference in the Bible to the most important part of the Sunday morning service, just before we all go home? 'Hebrews', obviously! More tea, vicar?

SEVENTH SUNDAY AFTER PENTECOST
July 28th 2019
Genesis 18: 20-32   Colossians 2: 6-19   Luke 11: 1-13
Psalm 138

CREATIVE GENEROSITY

As I have noted before, because we are only human, religious people inevitably make their gods in their own image, but usually without recognising or admitting that they are doing it. All the conventional ideas of God read as if we are talking about a human person who acts, thinks and speaks much as we do. Because that's the only language we have. Those who claim to 'know' all about God are just talking about themselves. They have to; we have no other basis to describe the indescribable. If you think you have actually got God all sorted, you have fallen into the trap. So we need to proceed with caution before anyone suggests that they have God all neatly tied up and that what they say comes directly from 'Him'.

That's not to suggest that we can never say anything about anything 'spiritual' or put forward any opinion. But it is a reminder that what we say comes from within, and only from within, human experience. A 'revelation' is a human insight that we have interpreted as a revelation. The words of God in the Bible are the words of men, (though there might be some by women here and there), even if they are claiming they come from God. It's their own interpretation of what happened in their mind, their thoughts, their experience.

This means that all our religious ideas are subject to change. What people thought about God in the past might not have been 'true'. We might now think something different. Nothing in life is unchanging; 'all things flow' (Heraclitus, 500BCE). Indeed, I would say that, in our culture especially, if Christian ideas do not change they will disappear. Faith is not about the static preservation of what was previously thought true; it is about the living reality of what is. What is alive changes. What does not change is dead.

So, to get to today's passages, is the source of all life and the sustaining power of the Universe really to be persuaded and bargained with like a reluctant MP who hasn't answered our emails? That was what they thought in OT times. The conversation between Abraham and God reads like a market trader and a customer haggling over the price of fish. Perhaps that's the kind of human experience that the old story grew out of. Like comparing God to a king, or a master or a powerful tribal chief it made sense at the time. Authority had to be bargained with to get what you wanted. Abraham has to persist in order to drag God's wrath down to a reasonable level and in the end God is reluctantly persuaded to do as he wishes.

Does your God need constant worship, sacrifices and prayers to appease Him? Is that really what He is like? This particular human representation of the way God behaves is frankly appalling. A morally righteous despot is perhaps the most dangerous kind. Even good people would suffer if this God had His way. Or is He just playing a power game with Abraham, as he was about (not) sacrificing Isaac, and the original price was never going to be required anyway? Surely that's just as bad?

Abraham knows that the wholesale destruction of everyone in the cities would be unjust, no matter what some had done. Admittedly that happens plenty of times elsewhere in the OT story where God is still presented as little more than a vengeful tyrant. But here at least is a reminder that while we might want to see right prevail and evil punished, like Inspector Javert in *Les Miserables*, we also need to have a sense of forgiveness and compassion or we are lost. Goodness can outweigh wrongdoing. That's the balance we try to strike, not only an emphasis on God making sure that the wicked always get their just desserts whatever the wider consequences.

In Luke's re-telling of Jesus' story, his version of God needs no persuasion. The ungenerous friend is the old idea rearing its ugly head again. In most of our human encounters, like Abraham, we want to help, to be generous. When my stepdaughter phoned me at 3.00 in the morning to come and collect her and her friend from a night club, I might have moaned, (a bit!) but of course I did it. It's what any caring parent would do.

So, says Luke's Jesus, don't think of God as behaving worse than you would yourself. His mind is not closed. Look and you'll make new discoveries. Ask and you'll find new answers. Things have changed, but you won't notice if you're not willing to risk the uncertainty that comes from moving on from the old ideas and images first. Faith is about opening up possibilities, not shutting them down.

So, I believe that Jesus' remembered emphasis on generosity should be reflected in the way we follow him today. If God turns out to be like it used to be said He was, then I'm in trouble! If Jesus' death really does make the only crucial difference between heaven and hell with final implications for my own eternal soul, then I'll have to take the consequences. But most people don't think it's true anymore so let's find something new to say to show that we aren't still stuck in the ancient past with the old idea of the reluctant God. Otherwise we're selling people short and not giving them what they deserve.

Paul is rather unhelpful here as far as I am concerned. He cautions his followers to treat what others tell you with care. But perhaps he is being overly-suspicious of new insights; maybe he's being just a little bit patronising. I suppose he wants to protect them during what he believed was the short time remaining before Jesus' return. But for all his talk about it, his understanding of the cross may have little or nothing to do with what actually happened on Good Friday, which is where I personally want to keep looking.

Does the traditional 'atonement' theology point to a God who still needs to be persuaded to be nice to us as before? I think this is the assumption Steve Chalke is challenging in his latest book on Paul for which he has received some criticism. Jesus 'had' to die, some say, to make it all happen and to satisfy God's requirement for justice. Even the idea of God's 'grace' seems to depend on a certain kind of faith first. If that's what we think it's all about, we have surely missed Jesus' radical point about everyone being welcome in the Kingdom? His was not the somewhat churlish 'God' of Abraham, nor often, in my view, the demanding 'God' sometimes preached in Christian churches.

Our idea of God, it is sometimes claimed, is unchanging. But the Old Testament law is not God's law. Paul's words are not God's words. The statements of the Creeds are not God's statements. Church institutions are not God's institutions. Everything is just *our* ideas and our structures. They grow as we do. The person of Jesus is where I would claim to see most evidence of 'Godness', even though he is only available to us through those who have taken his story and built upon it later.

'Turn your eyes upon Jesus' as the old chorus said. But not to avoid looking at 'the things of earth' as it also said, but to see them afresh and in an entirely different light. Perhaps we have buried the real Jesus under a mass of later ideas, like those put forward by Paul here, that have squeezed the creative life out of him, leaving only a hollow idol of a Christ, not a real human person who shows us how to live.

Perhaps theories of Jesus' supposed divinity have taken us far away from his offer of a generous Way, not beyond our humanity, but more deeply into it? Perhaps calling Jesus 'God' has distracted us from finding the truth about ourselves and turned it all into just another religion based on how to keep an ungenerous God sweet so that He will be nice to us in the end. If we cannot face up to that and be ready to change even our most treasured doctrines and beliefs, then maybe we have nothing left to say of any value and deserve to have it rejected. It's just a scorpion that stings, not a fish that feeds.

EIGHTH SUNDAY AFTER PENTECOST
August 4th 2019
Ecclesiastes 1:2, 12-14; 2:18-23   Colossians 3: 1-11
Luke 12: 13-21   Psalm 49: 9-11

JESUS THE TEACHER

If Jesus is not all about 'dying for my sins' and faith in him is not the gateway to eternal life, what is he about? Why do I still bother? It's a good question, and for many years I didn't. But the human journey takes us to many places and at this point I have the time and space to ask myself what it all means; and what *he* means in particular. I'm not sure you can do that without at least some engagement with the community of the faithful so, unlike many others, this particular prodigal is retracing his steps, if only to discover whether any of the old signposts still point in the same direction.

Everyone has to decide how to live. Most of the Bible story is about this life, not a supposed next one. That's one of the continuing attractions for me, rather than those religious traditions that see human life as a temporary trial to be endured and which doesn't really count for anything, before a hoped-for escape to something better. For me, earth, not heaven, is where Jesus belongs, as in Matthew's version of what we call the Lord's Prayer: 'Thy kingdom come; Thy will be done, on earth as it is in heaven'. (Have you ever noticed that the second part of that sentence is missing in Luke's version last week? We quote Matthew as the one Jesus taught, but we don't actually know. As they are different, maybe we should call each of these Luke's or Matthew's Prayer).

Finding the good in life should be our focus, not waiting for some heavenly alternative. But neither the writer of our OT passage, part of the 'Wisdom' literature, nor Paul in the Colossians passage, seem to agree with me. What depressing and dispiriting verses these are to cheer us up on a summer Sunday morning when we could have gone to the beach!

Life is either constant toil with no meaningful reward or legacy, or the world is going to hell in a handcart. Context must be relevant here. Life was tough in ancient times. Individuals must have felt extremely powerless. Paul thought that the end of everything was nigh and almost seems to revel in the depravity of it all in the meantime. It feels like he is saying that all races and nations are equally doomed; not that all are equally welcomed.

When we get to Lent and Holy Week we will focus, of course, on Jesus' suffering and death. But for now let's think about his life, and what it tells us about ours. That's the problem with relying on Paul. He knew little or nothing about Jesus and never quotes his teaching or parables. The story quickly moved on to something else: a message *about* Jesus, not the message *of* Jesus. We have admittedly limited access to what Jesus may have said and taught, at least in the first 3 gospels, which Paul didn't have. So we shouldn't waste it. Jesus' teaching has to be important in our discipleship, even recognising that it all comes to us at second hand, 'according to' the writer, not verbatim. But that's as close as we can get.

I've spent much of my life studying or working in education. My father became a teacher; my two brothers were teachers; I'm married to a teacher and my son is a teacher. Jesus, for me, is essentially a teacher. It's often the word that is used by others to address him, as in this gospel passage. John Churcher, a very helpful contemporary Christian thinker and writer, always talks of 'Rabbi Jesus'. I think it very likely that Jesus did undergo some formal training. (The gospel records disagree about whether he was himself a carpenter or known only as the son of one).

He seems to have had an extensive knowledge of the Jewish scriptures, way beyond that of other ordinary working people, and even beyond the official scholars, if often coming to radical new conclusions. Perhaps, like John Betjeman Jesus failed his final divinity exams because he was too interested in the 'inessentials' of faith!

We know enough to see Jesus as an unofficial Rabbi with a small family of followers who had a message to share about how best to live in order to reflect his God's ways. What he said was often controversial as far as the religious establishment was concerned. It got him killed. He was compassionate, inclusive, caring, often outrageous, even dangerous. The original message was not all about himself being on a par with God but about the 'Father' and His world.

What does a good teacher do? They don't just tell you things: 'information transferred from the notes of the teacher to the notes of the student without entering the mind of either'. (The Psalmist seems equally unimpressed by learning!) But good teaching changes you; it makes you *think*; it opens up new understandings, creative ideas and exciting opportunities. It gives you a perspective that you didn't have before. It sends you away fired up to do your own research in response.

And that's exactly what Jesus was remembered as doing with those who encountered him. A new angle on their sacred scriptures, which he wasn't afraid to re-interpret, and a new vision of their lives. The 'kingdom' or rule of God; right here, right now, not just a distant future hope. Not that the things he was remembered as saying were always very comfortable, especially to the complacent.

This passage is one of so many examples where Jesus seems to turn all existing ideas on their head. Life does not consist in the abundance of possessions – so much for wealth being a sign of God's blessing. But perhaps we also need to be cautious of being over-confident in our spiritual well-being. 'O God we Thank Thee that we are not like other people out enjoying themselves while we've made time to come to church today'. Is there such a thing as religious greed, not just material excess? The constant desire to save our own souls when perhaps we would do better to give them away?

We have to remember that the gospel writers, Paul and ourselves, all approach Jesus from this side of Easter. None of the gospels may give us Jesus' actual words, and I have to be especially cautious about John with his lengthy speeches in carefully-crafted Greek, a language that Jesus did not speak. But ordinary people seemed to have warmed to his approach and found his message about God's new rule/realm renewing and encouraging.

Those of us on the most radical humanist end of the Christian spectrum are sometimes accused of downgrading Jesus from Saviour to role model. We might argue that we have a different idea of 'salvation' as not about securing our eternal destiny, but about how to be fully human *now*, while we have the chance. Life doesn't last forever. But in the meantime, there is a world out there that needs us to be agents of his call for justice, peace and personal wholeness. That is the Jesus Way of bringing 'healing', (the same word in Greek as 'salvation').

Jesus isn't just an example from history; though he sits alongside those who also stood up to injustice and paid the price. He is a teacher and prophet; someone who makes us want to be like him. That's why his genuine humanity is so important, not just a put up job. Those whom he met were not 'saved' by his dying; they were inspired and healed by his living.

The 'imitation of Christ' is a long spiritual tradition but it can only be about following the human person of Jesus as much as we are able to find him. If he wasn't like us because he was some unique God among us, how could we ever be like him? So I believe I can still learn from what has been passed on about him. Not because he saves me from death, but because he offers me the chance to discover how best to live.

That is 'salvation' from the person I might otherwise have been. Discovering a personal wholeness by focusing on him. All the rest is ultimately unimportant. This is the Jesus we should be sharing with others; one who walks with us on our journey of self-discovery and who offers real hope for finding the only possible destination: our full humanity.

NINTH SUNDAY AFTER PENTECOST
August 11th 2019
Genesis 15: 1-6   Hebrews 11: 1-3 and 8-16
Luke 12: 32-40   Psalm 33: 12-22

KEEPING THE FAITH

'Faith is the assurance of things hoped for, the conviction of things not seen'.

Is faith 'blind', or should it have some logical, rational basis? One of the points of contention between many conventional believers and those who take a more radical approach is the extent to which the Christian message has to be compatible with what else we know as modern C21st grown-ups. Religions don't just have be 'true', they have to make sense.

Harry Williams in *The True Wilderness* wrote many years ago that nothing of any value could be said unless it is known to be true in our own experience. But then he asks 'What is truth'? And answers his own question by saying 'We cannot know'! We could be leading ourselves up the garden path but we can only ever hope to be true to ourselves. Absolute certainty is unhealthy and misleads us. Doubt is not the enemy of faith but a sign of spiritual health that spurs us on to new discoveries. Enjoy your doubts. Celebrate them. Use them.

The Church, from Paul onwards, has never been comfortable with uncertainty. From very early on it wanted to agree, or impose, Creeds and statements of faith which spelt out 'the' truth. Faith was seen as about signing up to convictions that were very much seen, written down and defined. These are the required beliefs. And woe betide you if you questioned them.

Many contemporary books and sermons suggest the same; this is 'the' truth, not just my version of it. The history of the Church is littered with the persecution of 'heretics'. But can anyone ever impose what *must* be believed on another person? Or is 'sharing in our faith' an invitation to join an adventure with a destination that is unknown, with a guide book that needs to be constantly updated and along a newly-trodden path we've never seen before?

I don't therefore see following the Way of Jesus as also requiring me to believe six impossible things before breakfast, as the White Queen in *Alice Through the Looking Glass* could manage. The Creeds contain what are for me, and for many others, a whole string of now unbelievable claims. There is no 'up' where God is or for Jesus to 'come down' from. The way in which he is said to have 'come down' as a human person is literally inconceivable! And so on.

I don't believe it because it doesn't meet the test of being true to *me*. That, in my opinion, is the problem with much so-called mission today. People are so often asked to set aside what they know to be true and adopt another idea of truth *instead*. 'Faith' is offered as an alternative set of understandings to the ones by which we normally operate. They are the 'world's way'. Believing in Jesus is said to be about having a counter-cultural mindset which asks us to leave the outside world at the church door first. It will never work, except for the few who want to be convinced, perhaps sometimes for entirely the wrong psychological reasons.

Jesus seems to be teaching here that, by contrast, his ways fit rather well with the way life generally is, though they aren't always easy to find. 'Look around you'. His examples are drawn from 'real' life; work, family etc. As we know, all gospel passages have a double life: then (Jesus' own life) and later (the community for whom the gospel was written 40 or more years afterwards). Is he 'the coming Son of Man' (from the book of Daniel) himself or was he expecting someone else? We don't know exactly what the term means and it has been a matter of great dispute for years, but it is entirely possible that it comes from Jesus himself. It makes sense to prepare for what may lie ahead; if we'd known the burglar was coming we would have made sure the alarm was on.

This has usually been interpreted as a call to put our lives in order, just in case. I have heard several sermons asking 'Are you ready'? There is a truth in living 'as if' time is short because it is, for each of us, as it was for Jesus. But I don't see this as being about an ever-repeated round of repentance and forgiveness in order to prepare for my eventual destiny in the future. I see it as more about engaging in a constant cycle of action-reflection to make the most of *now*. A permanent state of readiness for what will come today, tomorrow.

'The unexamined life is not worth living' said Socrates. Most of the time we drift through life without giving it a great deal of thought. But we should be always evaluating what we do;

the way we live; the values we hold etc. As everything else changes around us, and as we ourselves change, how do we keep our integrity, our honesty and our humanity? What 'worked' before may not be fit for purpose now.

So I am happy to ignore the annoying man in my local high street who shouts at me that I had better repent quickly because he 'knows' that Jesus is going to return a week on Thursday, or at least 'soon'. He is entitled, I suppose, to his version of 'faith', though not, in my opinion, to express it so aggressively. Both of us would, however, do well to take Jesus' point that you can never *know* what the future holds but life still requires us to decide how to live it. I don't know exactly where my journey is leading. Any decision to try and walk in Jesus' Way is a step on the road towards 'things not seen'. But faith also requires consistency with what we have found to be true.

So, for example, here are six rational facts I have hold on to.

(1) The Bible has a history; it was written by human beings like us, not dictated by God. We have learnt more since. (2) The Universe is billions and billions of years old and vast beyond our imagination, so the idea that we alone are at the centre of a Creator's master plan is just not credible. (3) Faith has to be compatible with what we now know about evolution and the laws of the natural world. (4) God is not male, old and living in the sky nor can he be persuaded to fiddle about with events if we ask him nicely. Things just happen. (5) Jesus was a real human being who lived and died as we do, not pretending to be like us as part of God's greater purpose. (6) The Church is

a human fallible institution that makes mistakes, can change its mind and cannot tell me what I must believe.

These are my own 'red lines'. Religious beliefs cannot require me to lay aside all logic and reason about the way things are as is often expected. To me, that isn't asking for an act of 'faith', it's just humanly impossible. That's why so many now ignore us or view the church as operating in an entirely different world that bears no relation to theirs. They are often right in their analysis. We cannot ask people to pretend they still live in the C1stCE or the C4thCE and expect to be taken seriously. We just look ridiculous if we do.

However, we may well still hold beliefs that seem out of step with some other contemporary values. There's nothing irrational in having faith in the power of goodness or love. Or in believing that I can be a better person or that the world can be a happier place. That's different. But maybe we do need to look in new ways first.

As Karen Armstrong has helpfully written in her work on Paul, 'having a faith' is also a statement of things that are 'hoped for'; a commitment, in the real world, to try and make a difference, and a desire to make those hopes a reality. It's not just about assenting to certain propositions as Christianity seems to have become.

'You can believe all the right things and still be a jerk' (Marcus Borg). If there are things we believe in but about which we cannot be certain, what are the things we hope for that we cannot yet see? The visions and values to which we are committed. We need to be constantly exploring that question as we discover more about what Jesus meant by the 'kingdom' and how it can change our view of the world. That's where we're going. Hold tight though. It might be a bumpy ride!

TENTH SUNDAY AFTER PENTECOST
August 18th 2019
Jeremiah 23: 23-29   Hebrews 11:29 – 12:2
Luke 12: 49-56   Psalm 82

DISAGREEING WELL

One of the worst of the old hymns, which thankfully we don't sing anymore, (and there are plenty of equally dreadful new ones), must be *Gentle Jesus, meek and mild.* Not only does it portray the believer as a simpering snowflake desperately low on self-esteem and self-confidence, but it also suggests that Jesus wouldn't say boo to a goose. I'm not saying that he should be portrayed like Henry V, armed and tooled up ready to fight his way to the kingdom of God – I don't much like *Onward Christian Soldiers* either.

But the Way of Jesus will sometimes lead to conflict. Way back on Pentecost Sunday I said that the 'spirit of holiness' unites. But that doesn't mean there is never any uncomfortable challenge in what we have to say or a hostile response to what we believe to be true. The Psalmist issues a sharp word to the powerful in God's name: '*How long will you judge unjustly and show favour to the wicked?*' That can't have gone down well.

That was, of course Jesus' own experience. His friends ran away or betrayed him it seems. He had enemies who ultimately conspired together to have him crucified. Why would anyone think that following him was going to be a safe quiet life? And the reality of conflict, both within the believing community and with powerful forces outside of it, is a constant background to the New Testament; both for the writer of this gospel passage and for the writer to the Hebrews. The Jews did not generally take kindly to those who now may have believed in Jesus as the chosen one. But the believers didn't agree too well amongst themselves either, especially once non-Jews started to join with their Gentile pagan ways.

And then there were the Romans who lumped them all together as irritating God-botherers and added plenty more crosses to that of Jesus, sometimes setting the bodies on fire to illuminate their splendid roads. Of course some of the faithful fell away once the going got tough. Those who were walking the Way of Jesus were a threat and not everyone could stay with it. I don't blame them. I would probably have done the same myself and kept my head down.

Jesus seems to have made it clear that going his Way will often be a challenge to the way things normally are. That's no surprise. Maybe if we never say or do anything that anyone else could object to, then we're not actually saying or doing anything worthwhile at all. So we shouldn't look to Jesus for a comfortable passage through life where everyone always gets along together. His message about the kingdom is radical, challenging to the status quo and may make people uncomfortable. We should expect controversy.

Quite rightly, Christians are often involved in protests and campaigns, even if they are unpopular or criticised as 'political'. (I wonder which ones Jesus would have joined?) One of the most controversial is the Israel/Palestine issue. The writer to the Hebrews seems to revel in the history of past conflicts. We are now living with the consequences of more recent battles over who has the right to live in the ironically-named 'Holy Land'. There's rather a lot of over-excited language here, as there often is today, but his point seems to be that, given all these past heroics, we shouldn't expect an easy time of it. Conflict is inevitable. Fair enough as far as it goes, but which side should we be on? That's a question each of us should seek to answer with as much integrity as possible.

The conflict that Luke has Jesus referring to is probably what was happening within his own church a couple of generations afterwards, as much as about what Jesus had encountered himself. The community of faith was in danger of breaking up. The younger people were rejecting the inherited faith of their elders because what they had been told had turned out not to be true. The world had moved on, not ended. But it was all getting tense; families were divided against each other, not just having a mild disagreement over Sunday lunch. Fellowship was being broken and opposing sides being taken up.

Such is the test of real community; we're not all the same. Genuine diversity means sharing with those who are different from ourselves, not seeking a ghetto of like-minded people. The best advice I was given when I went to University was 'Find a church that's just like this one. Then go somewhere else'. It's not easy; I have had to leave churches in the past because I felt so out of step, but a church made up entirely of people like me would be a disaster!

The Jeremiah passage also brings us back to conflict with one another. This might actually be more difficult to face than conflict with those outside. Much of what I have written in these notes would be completely unacceptable to many of those with whom I am travelling. Good Christian leaders have sometimes been forced out of their posts for suggesting that we need to let go of our old idea of God in order to find a faith that makes sense today. Others have only been able to remain in the Church at all by retreating to academic life and just writing incomprehensible books that few people actually read. I hope I have avoided both of those, though the second may well be true!

My old College Principal once suggested at a Baptist Union Assembly that Jesus was not the 'Son of God' in a literal sense and received regular hostile mail for years as a result. Some local churches wouldn't have us anywhere near them for fear of being contaminated. I shall probably get some pretty aggressive emails myself if certain 'Christians' ever read these reflections, (which they probably won't). I've virtually given up with Twitter; you just get angry criticism and self-justifying intolerance.

Of course I know I'm a non-conformist. I expect people to disagree with me. But dissent has rarely been welcomed as creative and renewing. The Church has not been good at listening to new ideas. But there is no hope for Christianity in the West unless we all accept that there is no one way of believing. The Church will not be effective or inclusive, as it must be, if it erects barriers that are too high for many to get over or if it is driven by a desire to impose one, (often very flawed) perspective on everyone.

How does the Church become more open to diversity? Not, I would argue, by watering everything down to just being 'nice' so that no-one can possibly disagree. We're back to 'meek and mild' again. There are many rooms in God's house and all should be able to find a place. There will always be differences; there must be if we are going be honest rather than just ignoring each other or secretly seething with hostility or feelings of rejection. But can we at least listen to each other and end up still on speaking terms?

Jesus is not a prize to be claimed by the 'gnostic' few who claim to have discovered the secret that the rest of us are too faithless to find. Divide and rule; 'I'm right and you're wrong', is not the way to engage with the modern world. I'm not sure Jeremiah is the best guide to how we should behave here. It's not that one view must be hammered home by the one faction that has God's approval. That will inevitably lead to the building being destroyed for everyone.

We seem to increasingly live in a culture where anyone who is 'offended' by something someone else says can demand an apology or the right to be protected from being exposed to hearing anything they don't agree with. As long as what is being said is not illegal, inciting violence, deliberately offensive, racist etc. I don't see why we can't all be a bit more thick-skinned.

Just as the irritant bit of grit in the oyster produces the pearl and the isolated voice crying in the wilderness might actually be right, surely the Christian family can cope with a variety of understandings and show a better way to the wider society? We have to learn to live with difference; even to celebrate it.

It may be that the name of Jesus is all we hold in common. But it's the built-in tension in a structure that keeps it standing. It doesn't make it fall down.

ELEVENTH SUNDAY AFTER PENTECOST
August 25th 2019
Isaiah 58: 9b-14   Hebrews 12: 18-29   Luke 13: 10-17
Psalm 103: 1-8

THE RHYTHM OF LIFE

Christians have a problem with the celebration of the Sabbath, including with what Jesus may have said about it. It was, and is, kept on Saturday, not on Sunday. So we don't have to observe it; we're not Jews. Those who argue that Sunday should be treated in exactly the same way, as a 'Christian Sabbath', are just making the idea up. Sunday doesn't have the same meaning.

There may still be an argument for keeping a day that is different from all the others. Take a break from mobile phones, email and social media. Shop workers are entitled to time off, families need an opportunity to get together etc. But I also remember the boring Sundays of my childhood when there was nowhere to go except church and nothing to do except Sunday School. I really wouldn't want to go back there.

So there are two issues here: First, what kind of day was the Sabbath now meant to be? Presumably this was an important issue for Luke's church to clarify as they hadn't all been Jews before. What was Jesus remembered as saying about it that was different from the usual Jewish teaching? What does that tell us about him, and about those who walk in his Way, rather than just about a day from a past tradition we don't actually follow? And second, what do Christians now have to say about Sundays and the modern rhythm of work and rest?

Let's start with the later Isaiah, Jesus' favourite prophet. Jews were expected to keep the Sabbath day 'holy'. It's there in the 10 Commandments. It was a recognition in daily life, reflecting the ancient Creation myth that God took time to step back and look at what He had made and to reflect on its goodness. If that was good enough for God then it was good enough for his people. It marked them out as different from other tribes and religions who had other patterns and rituals. But what does keeping the day 'holy' mean? Isaiah is pretty clear what his God is looking for.

The purpose of a holy day is to use it for the benefit of others, not for yourself. Spiritual discipline is always a good idea, and one that I'm not very good at. But it is not an opportunity to wallow in self-righteous self-congratulation but an invitation to use the time to recommit to meeting the needs of others. And this seems to have been what motivated Jesus. Sabbath ritual had become just that; done for its own sake alone as a test to weed out those who were less holy than they should be and enhance the status of those who took it all so terribly seriously.

Many of the characters in the Jesus story would have been very occasional Sabbatarians: shepherds, fishermen, 'sinners', tax-collectors, the sick and disabled, Samaritans, outsiders of all kinds. They would have had no chance of meeting all the various requirements or ticking all the liturgical boxes. 'Who cares'? says Jesus. It's how you use the day that matters. What better day to do some positive good, rather than just refraining from things and enforcing an atmosphere of compulsory misery?

Mark 2:7 has Jesus saying that the Sabbath was made for us, not the other way round. It's not that we have to fit in with what a God has decided we must do. It's that we have to use the day we have created in the right way. It's a blessing, essentially for others, not a curse that we have to endure.

In the Isaiah passage the prophet talks about removing the burden of Sabbath observance. Not pointing the finger at others for their lack of religious zeal, but satisfying the needs of the afflicted. So Jesus was spot-on in his interpretation. And the people loved it; one in the eye for the holier than thou brigade who think they are better than we are with all their religious ways. But the Calvary clock is ticking now. This was too much for those who were used to exploiting the rules to reinforce their own power. They'll be back!

So how can we use all this, accepting that Sunday is a day for celebration not a day just for making ourselves look more 'religious'? Firstly, by not criticising those who are not able join you. In the old days I was often greeted at an unfamiliar Baptist chapel where I was filling in for the regular Minister with 'we usually get more than this'. I always took this as a comment about me but it might equally have been aimed at the missing sheep.

People have busy lives, increasingly so. Perhaps our Sunday routine, largely inherited from previous generations when there wasn't much else on offer, is no longer fit for purpose. Weekdays might offer new opportunities now many people are not at work all the time or work just at weekends; times of services and meetings might need to change and be shorter, more focused.

Jesus seems to have often taken breaks from his ministry to recharge his batteries, alone or with his disciples. While he sometimes fasted, food was often involved it seems. No doubt some miserable Pharisee or other would have suggested that he could have been doing something more useful with his time. Showing people the Way of God's new realm wasn't all work work work. Re-creation needs to be written into our lifestyle.

When did someone at church last tell you not to come to a meeting, or even on a Sunday, because it was more important to have some relaxing quality time with your family or have a meal out with your friends? Discipleship is not measured by how long we spend on the 'sacred acre'. I never really understood that until I got a 'proper' job myself and could appreciate the juggling that might be required to always turn up to everything as I had expected others to do before.

And secondly, Isaiah talks about the Sabbath as an opportunity to offer food to the hungry. My local Sikh gurdwara always has free food on the go when anyone visits, and not just a lukewarm cup of tea and a stale biscuit. Of course some Christians won't eat it because it's been 'offered to idols'. Isn't refusing hospitality from others as bad as not offering it yourself? They also regularly take hot food out into the streets for those who need it and with no sneaky tract tucked into the naan!

The inclusive inner-city church that I sometimes attend has an open invitation for a meal every Sunday lunchtime, in-between the Eucharist and the service in Farsi. It seems to happen by magic; no complex rota or precious jockeying for position in the kitchen. Everyone is welcome even if you weren't at church before. People just volunteer to bring enough food for whoever turns up: Turkish one week, curry the next, Caribbean chicken the one after that. Not quite the feeding of the 5000 but just as much a 'miracle'.

Some of the community then have to go off to work or to other commitments. A day off may be a luxury for them. The first Christians would have had to fit their remembrance of Jesus around the first day of the working week. Sunday is not a Sabbath but maybe it might be a good idea to treat it as if it is, as long as it's Isaiah's and Jesus' version that we're following, not just an empty day always spent in endless services.

More broadly, this issue can also be seen an example of how the 'religious' and the 'secular' have to be constantly entwined, not kept separate. That's an entirely false distinction. Daily life is worship. Work is prayer. Service is discipleship. Every day is holy. (See 'Everything is holy now ', a song by Peter Mayer).

Perhaps we are moving into an age when the boundaries are becoming increasingly blurred and being 'Christian' for those who look to Jesus is just the same as being 'human' for everyone else. Not an escape from real life but a way of living it. If the believers can be open to that possibility, not keep telling us that we are 'out' and they are 'in', maybe his memory might yet survive and even flourish.

So there we are. This seems like a good opportunity to rest again and get ready for whatever comes next. Thank you for spending the time with me. Perhaps we will meet one day to discuss things further together. I am happy to speak at meetings and answer questions etc. on an expenses only basis.

For my latest rethinking about the search for a humanist spirituality inspired by the Way of Jesus, and to share your feedback, see:

www.ben-whitney.org.uk